SELF-MOTIVATION MASTERY

Using neuroscience, positive psychology, and emotional intelligence discover and develop your superpowers to master self-motivation

ANN HOLLAND, PHD

Library of Congress

Ordering information: Amazon.com, or Ann@StrivePerformanceCoaching.com

ISBN: 978-0-578-96377-8

Book Design by Alice Anderson

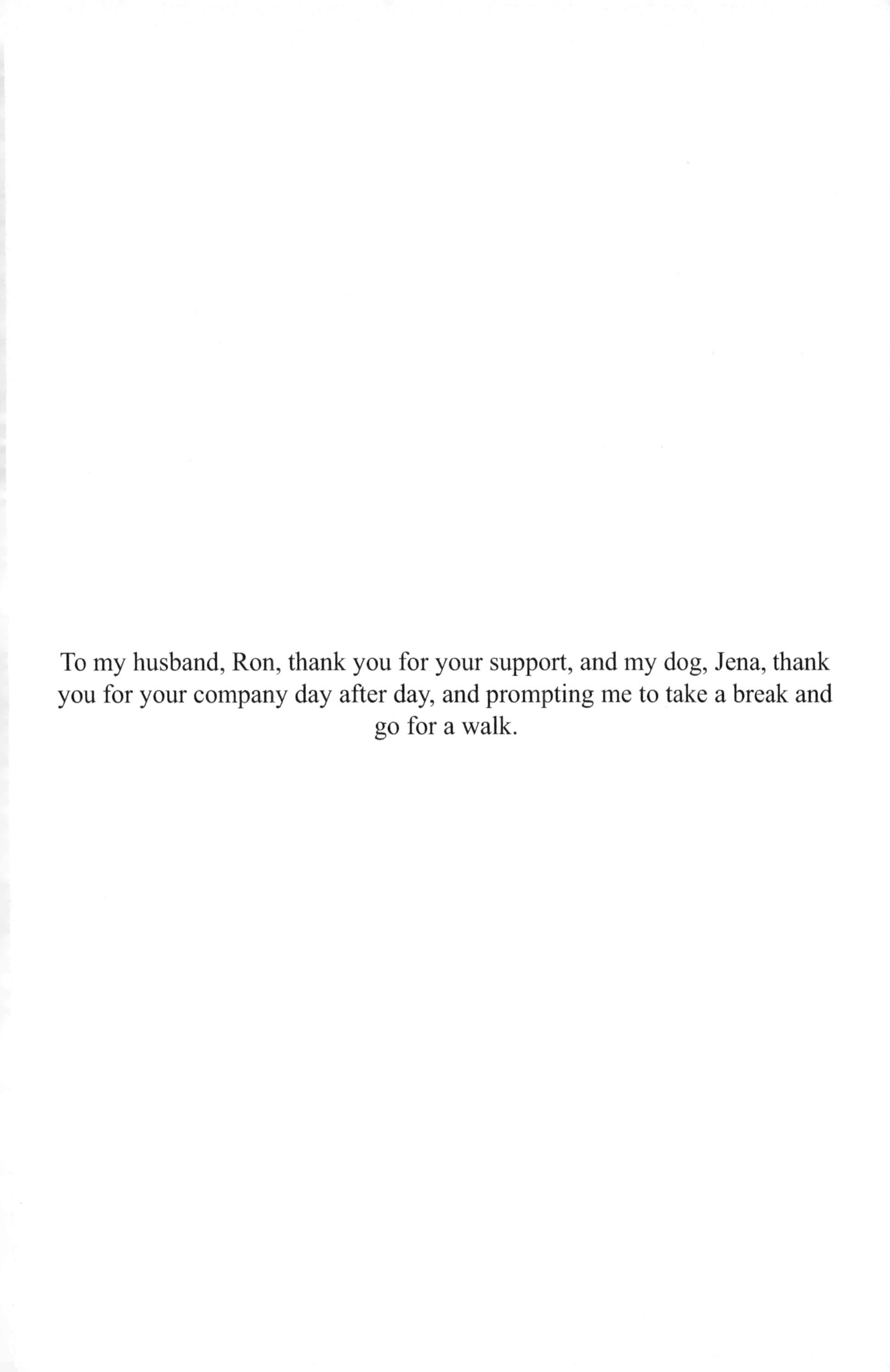

To my husband, Ron, thank you for your support, and my dog, Jena, thank you for your company day after day, and prompting me to take a break and go for a walk.

Contents

Foreword for Self-Motivation Mastery

by Mark Youngblood

When I first met Ann Holland, she was not at all what I expected.

I read her bio and saw that she had not one, but two master's degrees AND a Doctorate in Human Development… well I guess I expected someone who was going to be the stuffy academic type, and maybe a little bit arrogant.

She was none of those things.

Ann's warmth and humility were the first things I noticed about her. We chatted like old friends even though we had met only moments earlier. I liked her immediately.

Ann and I share a passion for empowering people to create the life they want. She told me that she loves "seeing the light bulb go off" when people gain powerful new insights. And she delights in helping people uncover the resources they already have inside to motivate themselves to fulfill their desires.

Ann is super smart and that comes through as soon as she starts to talk about her work. But she has the kind of "smart" that enables her to take complex topics and talk about them in ways that make sense to everyday people like you and me. That's one of the yardsticks I use to gauge if someone really knows their stuff.

This book is full of great suggestions and insights backed up by leading-edge neuroscience. It helps our understanding to know about that, but it can be overwhelming if someone talks in "geek-speak." Ann has a knack for explaining it in a way that enables us to understand it easily and put it to work powering up our motivation.

I have met many experts who write self-help books like this who have never really had to deal with the struggles and challenging life events that most of us do. And because of that, they couldn't really relate to their audience, and that showed in their writing.

So, I wanted to learn more about Ann's background, and what made her who she is today. What I learned could fill up a fascinating book all by itself.

You might not expect that someone with Ann's professional pedigree and many accomplishments started out in such difficult circumstances.

One of five kids, Ann grew up in federally funded housing in the Philadelphia area. And, unfortunately, like many young girls and women, she too suffered sexual offenses. In her teen years, her parents divorced and then some years later, she lost her father in a freak accident.

But despite those challenges, she determined that she would not let her environment define or limit her. And as a young adult, she left Philadelphia and set out to make her mark. The determination and inner strength she developed as a child helped her to succeed at achieving every major goal she set out for herself.

But even though she was very successful professionally, life kept throwing challenges her way.

At age 36, Ann endured the grief and loss of her first husband who was tragically killed in a car accident. And in the past several years, she stepped away from her career (and dream job) to care for her stepdad who was in the end stage of his life.

Yet each time, Ann bounced back and continued to pursue her dreams. Most recently, to write this book for you.

If life were smooth and the going easy, it might be much simpler to maintain our motivation and be super successful.

But it's not.

Life is a roller coaster. We can have many highs and many lows. And if we want to fulfill our heart's desires, we have to be able to motivate ourselves to keep going despite life's setbacks.

And Ann is a wonderful role model for that.

She isn't just teaching you how to find your motivation within yourself, she is showing you the way through the example of her own life.

Some of you may be early in your career or adult life and trying to figure out what you want. Others might have dreams and not know how to get started achieving them. And still others may have experienced setbacks and want help learning how to motivate themselves to get back on their feet and embrace what life has to offer.

This book has answers for each of you.

Ann told me that she had always wanted to write a book but didn't have the confidence to do it. She wrote down thousands of titles of potential books, but she could never get out of the gate. Until now.

Ann has always been passionate about learning why some people are motivated and others are not. She said that this topic "really floats her boat," and she realized that in her heart, this is what she went to school for. This is what she wanted to learn so that one day she could share it with you.

Today is that day. Enjoy!

“GO CONFIDENTLY IN THE DIRECTION OF YOUR DREAMS. LIVE THE LIFE YOU’VE IMAGINED.”

- Henry David Thoreau

INTRODUCTION

Discover Your Personal Path to Self-Motivation

A few years ago, I had a client who reached out to me because she was in a rut. She struggled to stay focused and felt disengaged from a job she had, up to this point, enjoyed. I will call her Mandi. Mandi was an emerging professional with high potential. I say high potential because I believe anyone who discovers their superpowers to master self-motivation has the potential to go confidently in the direction of their dreams and live the life they imagined.

After spending years working in organizations as a manager and leader, I have seen many *Mandies.* I left the corporate world to pursue the answer to the question: Why do some people seem to possess a bottomless pit of motivation while others need an extra push or a little more oomph of energy to stay excited and passionate? While our motivation to do our best for our family, friends, or our personal interests is likely to be high, sometimes staying motivated for our career or profession wanes from time to time.

Things can be challenging at work, leaving us feeling frustrated, out of sorts, or like we are in a rut, but it doesn't have to be that way. It's Mandi's success story that inspired me to write this book.

New research into the nature of the human brain reveals breakthroughs you can utilize to ignite your self-motivation to keep you engaged and enthusiastic. When that happens, your productivity improves almost organically. *Self-Motivation Mastery* will take you on a guided tour of this research, teaching you how to apply leading-edge science to your life, helping you achieve your personal best.

Chances are you've read books or attended classes, whether virtual or in person, about the importance of being a positive person. You may already know having an open, growth-oriented mindset can help you flourish not just personally but also professionally. It's common knowledge most people who succeed and move up in their careers are the ones who are self-motivated. You've read it in every rah-rah motivational book you've ever picked up, right? But all that excitement, cheering, and jumping up and down figuratively if not literally, can fade fast without a foundation to build upon.

Books imploring you to be a positive person have been around for almost a century. Although they may be interesting and fun to read, they have a problem: they fail to tell you how. It's not their fault, the science linking motivation to how your brain is hardwired didn't exist back then. That's why the "fake it 'till you make it" or repetitive affirmations such as "I am a motivated person" approach only lasts so long before you fall back into your innate behavioral patterns again. So, what if you're not a naturally self-motivated person, how do you get there? More importantly, how do you stay there?`

You'll find the answers to these questions when you understand the new brain science presented in this book. You'll discover what it takes to make the important shift from a person whose motivation is sometimes up and sometimes down, to a person with a steady flow of positivity and self-motivation, a zeal for life, and, yes, even your work. This is especially true if you're a person who's not in their dream job right now.

On these pages you'll follow the story of Mandi. Perhaps she's a lot like you. She likes her job and generally likes the people she works with, but she's fallen into a rut. Mandi learns the basics of leading-edge neuroscience, emotional intelligence, and positive psychology, which helps her begin to control her feelings and hence her behaviors. She also determines what drives her motivation, so she figures out her personal purpose. You will do the same.

In *Self-Motivation Mastery*, you'll learn just enough about the brain and the science behind motivation to understand what drives you. Each chapter offers activities designed to help you discover your own inner drive—self-motivation. If you work in an environment where you must dig down deep to find your motivation, keep reading.

If you work from home as so many people do now, you may miss the connection and energy that having coworkers around you provides. Or, if you work in a workplace where your co-workers are toxic to your sense of positivity, you may experience inertia. Discovering your personal path to self-motivation is more important than ever before.

For leaders, managers, and executives you'll discover you don't necessarily have to keep throwing out carrots to your employees, looking for external motivators like contests and bonuses to keep them performing at their best. External motivation makes people feel good temporarily and is the dopamine of achievement. But what comes next? You don't have to keep looking for ways to incentivize people. When employees come to understand how the brain works, how the mind works, and more importantly, how the brain and mind work together, they will recognize self-motivation can work to their advantage. When organizations are filled with motivated, engaged, and enthusiastic team members, the workplace has a focus and energy that translates into higher performance, retention, and productivity.

For business owners it's crucial that you're self-motivated and stay that way every day. If you're an entrepreneur, you started with an idea and a passion. But maintaining it can become a chore. After all, you're the driving force in your business. This book will be a guiding light to discovering your ability to becoming and staying motivated through the ups and downs of managing a staff and running a business.

I wrote this book because I want to help readers like you understand you have the ability to be and remain motivated. Self-motivated. I love seeing people succeed. I hope you aspire to great things and accomplish your dreams, whether they're professional or personal. Imagine if you could achieve your full potential, and then, go beyond. You may believe your potential is to reach a certain level. However, as you travel that road, there's a strong likelihood you'll come to realize you have special talents and unique gifts you didn't see before. When you're self-motivated you can do so much more than you ever thought was possible.

Over the years in my career, I often wondered why some people were motivated and others not so much. I wanted to help those who were less motivated to become more motivated because I was confident they would go farther and feel better about themselves and their results. I passionately believe that you don't have to let your current circumstances define you. The ability to become self-motivated is rooted deep within your brain and mind, and I wanted to unlock its secrets. If at some point down the road you find yourself in a rut again, it will be at a different level. If that occurs, I hope you'll return to these pages and re-discover your superpowers, so you become self-motivated once again and reach new heights.

As a coach and corporate trainer, I begin helping my clients by revealing to them the capabilities of their mind and getting to the root of what makes each person tick. What's exciting is scientists now know the answers to the questions about what causes that inner drive. When you make a few minor changes to the way you think and behave, you'll discover your own inner drive. I believe you have the ability to be a self-motivated person and accomplish your long-term dreams and desires.

Come along with me on this journey into discovering how your brain works, and how you can rewire the hardwire of your brain by taking control over how you think and behave. I hope as you read, you'll become inspired, confident, empowered, and act on it, which will help you perform at your best. Motivation is intrinsic, it's within you. Through my research, I've come to know you have so much more control over your destiny than you ever realized. It's time to discover your superpowers to master self-motivation! Are you ready to get started?

THE ROAD TO SUCCESS IS PAVED WITH MOTIVATION

CHAPTER 1

Power Up Your Self-Motivation

Are you on the road to a successful career? Not so much? Why not? What's getting in your way? What are you waiting for? Are you waiting for:

- Your company to provide the right incentive?
- Your manager to inspire you?
- The next job opening?
- The training department to offer you a leadership training class?
- The next great side-hustle idea to fall into your lap?
- All the stars to align?
- More importantly, are you getting in your own way?

If you're waiting for someone or something outside yourself for motivation, you may be getting in your own way. External motivation, often referred to as the *carrot* (incentives, praise, and rewards) and *stick* (pressure, punishment, and threats) date back to the 1940's when psychologist B. F. Skinner experimented with animals to move them to action using either treats or punishment. The sad thing is many people and organizations still rely on these forms of external motivation. It's not enough to simply wait for your company to provide some form of external motivation, someone to inspire you, or for something life changing to happen. Did you know motivation is something you can create from within? The best way to get unstuck and get out of your own way and on the road to achieving your goals is to power up your self-motivation.

Most people who dream of accomplishing important goals start with great passion and enthusiasm. However, over time, they lose momentum, energy, and drive. Why does this happen? It's easy to set a goal, we do it all the time. Staying motivated to achieve your goals, that's where it gets tough. Developing the skills to power up your motivation is where the rubber meets the road. Take New Year's resolutions, for example, according to a study at the University of Scranton, compiled by Statistic Brain, while nearly 93 percent of people set resolutions, less than eight percent of them actually summon their personal inner drive to follow through. Let's face it, we all get stuck and feel overwhelmed from time to time. I'm sure you've struggle with sustaining your motivation at times. Maybe you're experiencing that right now.

WHAT IF...

What if I said you can activate a switch in your brain that will enable you to feel charged-up, self-motivated, and raring to go?

What if I said you have the extraordinary ability to determine and achieve optimal levels of personal and professional performance as well as happiness when you feel self-motivated?

Both statements are true. Your brain has specific switches that trigger certain thoughts and actions. Once you understand

- how your brain works
- how your mind works, and,
- most importantly, how they work together,

you can make a conscious effort to gain control of your thoughts and feelings. You can literally change the programming and chemistry in your brain. This means you have the ability and power within your brain to become self-motivated. Professional success begins with personal growth. Personal growth is rooted in self-discovery, changing your thoughts and behaviors, and establishing new habits.

DISCOVERING YOUR SUPERPOWERS

With advances in psychology and neuroscience, we know more about the mind and the brain and how they work together synergistically than ever before. Neuroscientists have determined that your *state of mind* is rooted in this physical, electromagnetic, quantum, chemically based mass called the human brain. Furthermore, they've discovered your brain can turn on and off switches that trigger the direction of your motivation. You discover your superpowers by learning to turn on and off the switches in your brain.

I invite you to follow along with my client, Mandi, as she describes her journey of self-discovery.

MANDI'S JOURNEY TO DISCOVERING HER SUPERPOWERS TO MASTER SELF-MOTIVATION

JANUARY 2ND

Another holiday season full of celebrations has come and gone. Another year of fattening foods and high-calorie drinks under my belt. Arghhhh, truth be told, I need to loosen my belt a notch…maybe two. Oh well, once again, I'll declare this year as the year I'll lose weight and get in shape. Yep, that's my New Year's Resolution. Yay!

JANUARY 3RD

The marketing blitz is on. Everywhere I look I see advertisements, coupons, and a ton of incentives for fad diets and gym memberships. Every year, I, along with millions of other people who overindulged during the holidays, are now faced with additional pounds above or below the belt. In unison, we sound the battle cry once again… it's time to lose some weight. Oh, and there are still Christmas cookies in the fridge.

JANUARY 4TH

Following the advice of many books I've read over the years on how to successfully lose weight and get in shape, and obtaining the approval of my doctor, I've set my goals, mapped out my food plan, and come up with a well-rounded workout program. This year, I've even enlisted my neighbor, Marcy, to be my walking buddy. Fitness gurus widely encourage most people of my size and age to set a goal of losing one to two pounds a week. Marcy said she's going to hang her dream bathing suit she hopes to wear on vacation to Acapulco next spring on her closet door to provide a visual reminder of her goal. I think I'll do the same. I have a cute, yellow sleeveless summer dress I bought three years ago in my closet. The tags are still attached. That speaks volumes about my intentions versus my results when it comes to losing weight.

JANUARY 5TH

Today's my first day back to work after the holidays. Everyone is buzzing with stories about their holiday break and how they spent their year-end bonus. My boss surprises the team with donuts and coffee. He wants to inspire us to regroup and get energized to meet the company's annual goals. My first hurdle…donuts…really! Doesn't he know almost everyone on the planet starts a diet this time of year?

The voice in my head begins its incessant chatter:

Okay Mandi, how do you get past the donut tray without taking a single donut? Well, maybe, I'll just take one. I'll look for the smallest one, or one without icing. No, that's no good. A donut is about 350 calories. I just won't have a donut at all. But then everyone will ask me why I'm not eating a donut. Then I have to explain myself. I'm on a diet. Arghhhh, how cliché! I know, I'll have a donut, so they see me as part of the team. I just won't eat lunch. Oh, that won't work either. I'm having lunch with a vendor today. They're taking me to Spenellies, my favorite Italian restaurant. They make lasagna to die for, besides, he's picking up the tab.

And what will I do on Friday when our team meets for its weekly, company-

mandated teambuilding pizza-fest? Maybe I'll find an excuse to get out of it. I don't like those meetings anyway. As a matter of fact, I don't even like my job anymore. Maybe this is the year to look for a new job. I just don't feel motivated to get my work done. I need help!

FEBRUARY 12TH

Well, the diet and exercise program are going more slowly than I hoped. After six weeks, I've only lost three pounds. Marcy hurt her foot, so she dropped out as my walking buddy. As a result, the only walking I've done is from the front door to the mailbox. Honestly, I really enjoy sleeping in that extra 30 minutes in the morning.

Work has settled back into a normal routine. Each morning I "check in" at the office coffee station and fill up my favorite mug. The one with a big yellow smiley face that reads, "**have a nice day**." Then, I meander back to my workstation. I scan Facebook, LinkedIn, Instagram, and Twitter for "breaking" news. Then I fumble around on TikTok for any funny video clips I can find. Sooner or later, I see selfies posted from friends and family having fun and enjoying life, while I'm sitting in my "spacious and attractively decorated" cubicle. Then I check emails, phone messages, and scan my social media accounts once more before psyching myself up to finally start another day's work. Let's face it, I am totally unmotivated. I need help.

MARCH 15TH

Ring! Ring! "Hello this is Ann. How may I help you?"

"Hi, this is Mandi. I need help alright! I just can't get myself motivated. Can you help?"

"Okay, Mandi, tell me a little bit about your situation."

"I've tried everything from goal-setting, to writing out my plans, to posting visual reminders and affirmations. I've even tried enlisting the support of others, but I can't seem to make progress on my personal goals or get the work done I need to do in my job. What the heck is wrong with me? How can I get motivated?"

Sound familiar? If you're like most people, you probably recognize some of the same challenges Mandi faces. She had the best of intentions to lose a few pounds and get in shape. She was inspired as many people are with the trigger of a new year's resolution. Mandi did many things right, she

- set a SMART goal: it was specific, measurable, achievable, relevant, and timebound;
- researched and developed a well-thought-out plan of exercise and healthy eating habits that was appropriate for her age, size, and general health;
- enlisted support from her friend Marcy;
- identified a visual trigger to remind herself to stay on track (yellow dress); and,
- linked the emotional feeling of being healthy and fit with her goal of losing weight and getting into shape.

So, what went wrong? Mandi not only feels stuck in her effort to get in shape, she's in a downward spiral at work. She is easily distracted and feeling discourage and unmotivated. As a motivation coach, I have worked with many clients like Mandi, who have good intentions and positive attitudes only to find themselves faced with challenges and setbacks that throw them off track. Once the external sources she depends on fall apart, she struggles to sustain her motivation. Setbacks, missed opportunities, and derailments can happen to anyone when they're striving to achieve personal and professional goals. Let's take a deeper look into motivation, what it is and how it works, and, like Mandi, you too will experience a motivation breakthrough!

MOTIVATION: TO BE MOVED INTO ACTION

Consider motivation as a journey that takes you to an end-state or the destination you choose. In the context of this journey, motivation means, "to be moved into action." Motivation is different for each person, and it can be different in various phases of your life.

Consider the Tiger Woods story:

▶ Tiger Woods

From early childhood, Tiger Woods dreamed of becoming a professional golfer. His dream was not just to be a pro golfer, but to be one of the best golfers in the game. By age 15, he was the youngest U.S. Junior Amateur champion. Woods graduated from Western High School in Anaheim, California at age 18 and was voted "Most Likely to Succeed" in his graduating class. At 19, Woods participated in his first PGA Tour in 1993. By age 20, he was the first golfer to ever win three consecutive U.S. Amateur titles. During the first decade of his career, Woods was the world's most marketable athlete. In 2021, Forbes reported Wood's net worth was in excess of $800 million.

Did you know Tiger Woods stuttered as a boy? He took classes to help him manage his stuttering. He talked to his dog for hours as practice to overcome it. As an accomplished professional golfer, Woods has had to overcome several setbacks in his personal life including medical challenges. Each time he's returned to the game with vigor and determination. Tiger Woods is widely regarded as one of the greatest golfers ever, and one of the most famous athletes of all time. Woods discovered his personal path to self-motivation at a young age. His ability to look inward and tap into his personal superpowers to becoming self-motivated and sustaining that motivation throughout his career has been one of his most valuable skills.

THE FIRST STEP TO DISCOVERING YOUR SUPERPOWERS

Everyone's path to success is unique. There are countless stories like Tiger Wood's story about athletes, celebrities, monks, entrepreneurs, corporate executives, and more. Each one has found their inner source of motivation and tapped into it. They have mastered self-motivation by using their superpowers.

The first step to discovering your self-motivation superpowers involves becoming self-aware. When you have a better understanding of yourself, you're able to experience yourself as the person you truly are. The more you know about yourself, the better you will become at setting intentions and overcoming barriers specific to your life experiences and desires. Self-awareness is empowering and is one of your superpowers!

ACTIVITY #1

SELF-AWARENESS: WHAT MOTIVATES ME AND HOW DO I GET IN MY OWN WAY?

Ask yourself the following two questions: A) What motivates me, and B) How do I get in my own way?

WHAT MOTIVATES ME?

Instructions: Rate how each of the following motivating factors energize you to act: *On a scale of 0 to 10 rate the factors that energize you to act. A score of 0 means it doesn't energize you at all up to a 10; a score of 10 means it energizes you more than anything else to take action.*

1. ACHIEVEMENT: Achievement is about accomplishing a goal. It can include factors like career advancement, completing a task, getting a promotion, or meeting a deadline.

0 1 2 3 4 5 6 7 8 9 10

2. PERSONAL SUCCESS: Personal success is about fulfilling those desires related to your lifestyle, values, and belief systems. It can include having balance in your life, family time, having a sense of security and stability, being your personal best, having freedom or independence, or simply experiencing peace and happiness.

0 1 2 3 4 5 6 7 8 9 10

3. MASTERY: Mastery is about being the best at what you do. These factors can include engaging in competition, being an expert, breaking records, or reaching the top of your profession.

0 1 2 3 4 5 6 7 8 9 10

4. SELF-INDULGENCE: Self-indulgence is about your ego. It can include your desire for money, attention, fame, power, winning, and control.

0 1 2 3 4 5 6 7 8 9 10

5. PURPOSE: Purpose is about having a sense of internal meaning to what you do in life. It can include factors such as leaving a legacy, altruism—helping others, having a positive impact or driving change, being relevant, self -actualization, or finding enlightenment.

0 1 2 3 4 5 6 7 8 9 10

6. RELATEDNESS: Relatedness is about being connected to others in a positive way. It includes social connectivity, feelings of acceptance, a sense of belonging, and attachment to other people, teams, projects, or movements.

0 1 2 3 4 5 6 7 8 9 10

7. AVOIDANCE: Avoidance is a part of human nature. It's about moving to action to avoid a negative consequence such as feeling shame, anxiety, humiliation, or fearing failure, punishment, or the loss of something you value.

0 1 2 3 4 5 6 7 8 9 10

8. OTHER: What motivates you that is unique to you?

0 1 2 3 4 5 6 7 8 9 10

HOW DO I GET IN MY OWN WAY?

Instructions: Check each of the barriers that get in your way of getting your work done.

____Procrastination (putting off until tomorrow what I could do today)

____Distractors (I find myself avoiding what needs to be done by looking for other things to do like scanning social media or watching TV when I should or could get work done)

____Lack of organization (I don't have what I need, or, if I do, I can't find it under the pile of paper on my desk)

____Lack of confidence or self-esteem (feeling anxious because I lack the competence to get the job done, or fearing I may fail in what I try to accomplish)

____Boredom (what I'm doing lacks challenge, or I'm simply uninterested in what I'm doing)

____Lack of enthusiasm (I'm not energized because what I'm doing ranks low on my "what motivates me" scale)

____Lack of energy (I'm physically, mentally, or emotionally fatigued)

____Lack of goals (I really don't know what I want in my life or career)

____External factors (resources or other factors that may be out of my control)

____Fear (fear of failure, fear of change, fear of not being good enough, or fear of the unknown)

____Waiting for someone or something to inspire me.

____Perfectionism (I cannot move on until everything is just perfect)

____Feeling overwhelmed (so much to do, I don't know where to start)

Now, list the top three motivation factors energizing you to act.

1. ____

____

2. ____

____

3. ____

____

List the top three barriers that get in your way of getting things done.

1. ____

____

2. ____

____

3. ____

____

KEY CONCEPTS

- ✓ Are you on the road to a successful career? If not, why not? What gets in your way? It's not enough to wait for the company to provide external motivation, someone to inspire you, or for a life-changing event to happen. Motivation can be created from within. The best way to get out of your way and achieve your goals is to power up your self-motivation.

- ✓ Staying motivated to achieve your goals is where the journey gets tough. Developing your skills to power up your motivation is where the rubber meets the road.

- ✓ When you understand how your brain and mind work, you'll realize you have an inner power to motivate yourself. You can shift your motivation from depending on external influences to becoming self-motivated; mastering your ability to create internal motivational drivers.

- ✓ Motivation is a journey that transports you to the end-state or destination of your choice. For the purpose of this journey, motivation means, "to be moved to action." Motivation is different for each person, and it can be different in various life phases.

- ✓ The more you know about yourself, the better you will become at setting intentions and overcoming barriers specific to your life's experiences and desires. Self-awareness is empowering and is one of your superpowers.

YOUR NOTES:

MOTIVATION IS THE ORIGIN OF DETERMINATION

CHAPTER 2

What is Motivation Anyway?

APRIL 1ST

"Well Mandi, you did a great job completing the self-awareness activity. Now you're ready for the next step in discovering your superpowers to master self-motivation," I said, confidently.

Mandi replied, "Before moving to the next step, I have a question for you, Ann."

I said, "Okay, Mandi, fire away!"

She asked, "When did you first discover your superpowers to become self-motivated?"

I smiled, "That's a fair question, Mandi. I'm happy to share my story."

MY STORY

As a young child, I lived in a government-funded project known as Lacey Park in Warminster, Pennsylvania. Dad was in the military and overseas more than he was home. Mom did her best to raise three kids under the age of eight with a fourth child on the way. We were quite poor. However, I didn't know it until I went to school.

The night before my first day of school was like Christmas Eve for me. Instead of dreaming about tearing into wrapping paper concealing what I hoped was a new ragdoll, I dreamed of picture books, meeting my new teacher, running toward the swings and monkey bars laughing with new friends, eating lunch in the cafeteria, and, of course, riding the school bus. I remember it like yesterday; Bus Number 5. The school bus driver was a plump, jolly man named Hoppy. He sure was friendly, always giving me a smile, a wink, and a wave as my two older brothers boarded the school bus before I started school.

Finally, it was my turn to climb up into the bus and head across town to start school. This was my big day. It didn't turn out quite as I imagined. It became obvious on the first day of school; I wasn't like the other kids. My clothes were clean, but they weren't new. Other girls wore store-bought dresses with matching bows in their hair. The boys donned new trousers and bright white sneakers.

At lunchtime, we lined up to make our way to the cafeteria. I couldn't help but notice most of the other kids carried shiny new lunch pails that flashed pictures of superheroes like Batman and Barbie. As I sat alone at the end of what seemed like a mile-long lunch table, I watched them snap open their lunchboxes and pull out a Thermos that matched. It contained a sandwich bulging with lunchmeat and American cheese, a mini-sized bag of Lays potato chips, and an apple. Embarrassed, but still hungry, I reached for my peanut butter and jelly sandwich made with the heels from the ends of a shrinking loaf of bread. Instead of a shiny, new lunch pail, my mom in her resourceful, repurposing efforts stuffed my sandwich in the plastic bread bag. Most mothers would discard such bags as used up trash, not my mom. She saw at least one more good use for the bag. I understood at that point, we were poor. I realized I probably wouldn't be accepted into a circle of lunch buddies.

This was the first of many epiphanies, where I discovered I couldn't allow my circumstances to define me. I figured I'd have to dig deep and find a way to walk down the bustling hallways with my head held high. I was determined to not only survive the experience but thrive. That was my first lesson in developing self-esteem and understanding self-motivation. I knew I'd need to find strength within me to move forward with determination. I didn't realize it at the time, but this was the beginning for me in discovering my superpowers to mastering self-motivation.

As my mom read fairytales to me as a little girl, I dreamed of going to school so I could learn to read. Learning and knowledge are my primary motivating drivers. An inner voice spoke to me, encouraging me to always put my best effort forward. Yes, I wanted to fit in like most children, but the excitement of learning drove me to persist beyond my discomfort about not fitting in and make the best of the opportunity school presented. That lesson and my passion for learning remained with me from first grade all the way through earning a Ph.D.

You see, Mandi, motivation is a source of determination. Let me explain what motivation is and how it works.

MOTIVATION IS A JOURNEY

Think of motivation as a journey that takes you from where you are, your current state, to where you want to be, a future state. According to 19th century German philosopher Arthur Schopenhauer, motivation means to *move into action*. Motivation deals with internal and external factors that stimulate energy within to exert persistent effort, attaining your desired end-result. In other words, motivation energizes you to act. It's the mother of all action. It results from the interactions between conscious and unconscious triggers linked to internal influencers including your desires and needs. External factors that motivate us can include incentives, rewards, and goals. Our internal state or condition activates behavior and drives people to create positive outcomes or to avoid negative events. Motivation involves biological, emotional, social, and cognitive forces that activate behavior. It's the *why* behind what drives human action. For example:

- Hunger will drive a person to raid the refrigerator, satisfying a biological and maybe an emotional need for food.
- Loneliness will drive a person to reach out and connect with others. This satisfies psychological, emotional, and social needs.
- A student pays their school loan on time, so they aren't slapped with a late charge, fulfilling a desire to avoid punishment.
- A person reads a book about a subject they're interested in to gain knowledge which gratifies a cognitive need to learn and grow in personal knowledge.
- Playing on a team sport satisfies a person's need to be physically fit, emotionally bond with their teammates, be valued as a contributor, and win the game. Sports satisfy both biological and psychological needs. When a team member contributes successfully to a team win, they avoid getting cut from the team, placating the need to avoid a negative event.
- Although people are driven to work for different reasons, the workplace provides

> personal or professional fulfillment. Some people work because they love their work. Others work to accomplish goals or feel as if they are contributing to something larger than themselves. Some enjoy the challenge work provides, and others desire the sense of belonging and camaraderie. Some people are driven by compensation whether it is a salary, bonus, benefits, or other perks. Let's face it, one of our essential needs is to provide for ourselves and family.

As you can see, what drives people is individual and diverse. However, at the end of the day, there is an internal force at work to satisfy a desire or need that drives a person's behavior.

An award-winning entrepreneur and inventor, Joy Mangano has a reported net worth of $70 million. She made it despite humble beginnings. A divorced mother of three, she held a variety of jobs including waitress and airline reservations manager to make ends meet. After growing frustrated with ordinary mops to do her chores at home, she designed the Miracle Mop, a self-wringing plastic mop. With her own savings and investment from family and friends, she made a prototype and manufactured 1,000 units. She peddled her invention at trade shows and local stores. However, her desire was to mass produce her invention and sell it nationally. She felt strongly it would help moms everywhere. After several attempts to get the attention of QVC to sell her mop on television, she was granted an on-air spot. She sold 18,000 mops in 20 minutes.

Mangano went on to invent a variety of successful products, including Huggable Hangers, Forever Fragrant, and Clothes It All Luggage System. She is named inventor of 71 patent families and 126 distinct patent publications. She is considered the Home Shopping Network's most successful inventor, with annual sales of over $150 million. Clearly, Mangano was driven for her own unique reasons. The end result? She was moved to action and achieved her desired goals.

A variety of driving forces can activate behaviors to satisfy a need or achieve a desired end-state. Mangano's story demonstrates how internal and external motivational factors stimulate energy within to exert persistent effort, attaining your desired end-result.

MOTIVATION BEGINS WITH INSPIRATION

I've found people often use the terms "inspiration" and "motivation" interchangeably. Frequently, people think these two words mean the same thing. However, that's not true.

- Inspiration is the awakening of a state of mind. Perhaps something touches you in a way that excites within you a desire to do something. Inspiration is the creation of a motive or a deeply held reason or desire to move you to act.
- Contrast this with motivation, the process of moving into action.

One of America's greatest inventors and businessmen, Thomas Edison once said, "Genius is one-part inspiration and ninety-nine percent perspiration." While there's a tremendous value to the latter, the former sets the wheels in motion. I would add the 90 percent perspiration is achievable through motivation. Let's take a closer look at inspiration.

Inspire comes from a Latin word which means to inflame or blow into. When you inspire something, it's as if you're blowing air over a low flame to make it spark and grow. It means to excite, encourage, or breathe life into a thought or an idea. It's the stimulation or arousal of your mind, your emotions, or your state of belief. Being inspired can help you chase your dreams with enthusiasm. It's living in a state of mind where everything seems possible. It's about believing in yourself, shifting your mindset from thinking *impossible* to *I'm possible,* as Oscar-winning actress Audrey Hepburn famously said. We find clarity, purpose, and the enthusiasm to start doing something when we become inspired.

Inspiration is highly personal. The same event can impact people differently, for instance, watching the Olympics could inspire someone to:

- Take up a sport or become a fan of a sport you didn't follow before.
- Begin a fitness and weight loss program.
- Travel to other countries – particularly one where the Olympics was held.
- Swell with patriotic pride and get involved in a movement or event that helps your country or community such as putting on a local fundraising event for Special Olympics.
- Become motivated to achieve something you desire personally or professionally as you watch Olympians overcome obstacles and move forward with determination.

Many people believe inspiration is only found externally. It happens when a stimulus causes a state of arousal. However, science reveals you don't have to wait for someone or something to be struck with a bolt of inspirational lightning. You can find your own inspiration once you discover your superpower – self-inspiration. If you wait for your manager or a motivational speaker to inspire you, you could be waiting a long time. Meanwhile, waiting can leave you feeling stuck and unproductive. Lacking inspiration can be the root cause to procrastination such as scanning your social media multiple times to avoid getting started with your workday. Our understanding of cognitive behavior demonstrates behavior affects how you think and feel. Conversely, how you think and feel affects your behavior. Inspiration is a pathway to change your way of thinking, feeling, and behaving.

I asked Mandi, "What triggered you to want to lose weight and get in shape back in January?"

"Well, Ann, after the holidays came and went, I didn't feel good. I felt like I was lagging physically and mentally. I didn't like the direction my health and well-being were heading. I've always been active, and I like being engaged. I enjoy taking the lead, putting together social activities and work projects. But I felt like I was bogged down. I was sluggish physically, and I felt mentally disengaged. I didn't feel like myself. As I think about it, that's probably why I'm also frustrated at work," she said with a sigh. "I like my job and the people I work with. I just don't feel energized."

I acknowledged her, "Thanks for being honest and taking a careful look at what's going on. While some people find inspiration *within* like you described, from observing what's happening in your psyche and how that affects your physical and mental well-being, others may see an image or hear a message or experience another external trigger that causes them to move in to action. Some people establish a goal of losing weight so they can wear a certain size clothing. Or a goal to hike the Grand Canyon can be an external trigger to get in shape. The same concept applies at work. For some, an internal desire or aspiration to get promoted, achieve a higher status, or become known as an author propels them. The key is, whether you're internally inspired by observing your own desires or needs, or you're inspired by an external trigger, an internal conscious or unconscious thought triggers your brain and mind to move into action."

We all have underlying triggers in our conscious and unconscious mind that fire based on our internal desires and needs as well as external incentives and rewards. There are steps you can take to find your inspiration within. First, be willing to open your mind to possibilities. Find your quiet space. Let your mind get quiet and allow space for new ideas to ignite. Many people find being in nature gives them an opportunity to let their mind relax and receive new thoughts. Others find success in meditation, and I think everyone's had a few epiphanies while taking their morning shower. To find your personal source of inner inspiration form an intention. Consider asking yourself questions when you're in your quiet space like:

- Where do I find my energy?
- What excites me?
- What's my purpose?
- If I had no obstacles in my way, what would I do?
- What do I value most in my life or career?

WHAT DOES SCIENCE SAY ABOUT MOTIVES, DRIVE, NEEDS, DESIRES, AND INCENTIVES?

Scientists, philosophers, and psychologists have searched for centuries to discover the answers to questions like:

- What's the difference between motives, drive, needs, desires, and incentives?
- Do personality traits affect motivation?
- Why do some people seem more driven than others?

To understand motives, start by having a clear, realistic picture of what makes you tick as a human being.

Although human nature matters, it's not the end all be all of motivation. The term "human nature" refers to the essence of humankind, or what it means to be human. As human beings, most of us share certain psychological, emotional, and behavioral characteristics. Humans also have basic physiological and psychological needs, which are an important part of human nature. These needs act as motivational drivers. How you satisfy these needs can vary based on personality traits, environment, and possessing a desire to act to satisfy your needs. Let me break it down.

There are three categories of human needs. The first two categories are basic needs: physiological needs and psychological needs.

Physiological needs refer to deficits that exists in the material body. They include the basics of food, water, and shelter.

Psychological needs, however, don't have any material existence. They're mental or emotional in nature. Psychological needs include affection, security, and self-esteem. Basic needs are considered deficiency needs because if they aren't met, you're likely to strive to make up the deficiency.

The third category of needs is referred to as higher needs or growth needs. It addresses the need to achieve self-fulfillment. This group can include the need to learn or contribute knowledge, experience a sense of self-acceptance, and achieve a sense of peace.

Psychologist Abraham Maslow suggested human needs were arranged in a hierarchical order. He based his theory famously known as the *Hierarchy of Needs* on the premise that basic physiological needs or security needs must be satisfied first. Psychological needs come next. Maslow proposed as security and psychological needs are met in his pyramid-shaped hierarchy, higher growth needs become important. Keep in mind, a person can move in and out of a particular level on the hierarchy of needs throughout their life.

Motivation reflects the uniqueness within each of us. It energizes us to gain what we value as desired outcomes like improved performance, personal growth, or a sense of purpose. Desires are personal and driven by our personality, talents, and disposition. However, certain fundamental drives, needs, and incentives are considered universal in our physical and psychological makeup.

Drive moves a person to satisfy a *need* or pursue an aspiration (*desire*). You probably dream of success, but what moves you to act, persist, and execute to achieve your goals? How do you reach a level of achievement such as being the master of your craft, a top athlete, a popular performer, or a CEO? Or, how do you achieve self-actualization?

Some argue success is about fame, money, a desire to win, or being recognized as the best at what you do. These things drive many people. There can be an external *incentive* (the carrot) that pushes you to accomplish a goal. However, without an inner force, most people are still living in the dreaming stage, wishing and hoping for success.

Drive is an inner force that compels us toward achievement. Fame, money, and recognition are learned external incentives determined by our environment. They stimulate our desire to rise in status. However, *drive* is an innate part of human nature. It's activated by what we perceive as a gap between what we have and what we want. It's a motivation triggered by the deprivation of a physiological or psychological need, or a desire we want to satisfy. This makes goals setting incredibly valuable. It helps us establish where we are and where we want to be.

The value and importance you attach to satisfying a need or achieving a desire determines your drive. If you're stranded on an island with no apparent rescue at hand, you'll experience an intense drive to forage for food, water, and shelter. This inner force comes naturally because your brain triggers your desire to survive.

Golfing great Tiger Woods is a person who's looked within to discover his personal drive to achieve his goals. Woods valued his dream so passionately he was stimulated to move into action and pursue his goal with great intensity. He overcame obstacles and setbacks and achieved his dream of becoming one of the best golfers of all time.

In your career, you may be driven to move up the corporate ladder to an executive level or own your own business. This drive provides motivation to increase productivity, boost innovation and creativity efforts, build networks and relationships with colleagues, and become more committed to your work and overall performance. Consider your aspirations and what is driving you in your career.

PUSH AND PULL MOTIVATION

Motivation is driven by the anticipation of future outcomes, which can be either positive or negative. It comes from internal sources that push us and from external sources that pull us forward. Internal sources link us to satisfy basic physiological and psychological needs. External sources link us to environmental incentives. An incentive is an anticipated environmental feature such as wanting a reward or avoiding punishment. It pulls us toward what we want or away from what we don't want. A positive reward attracts us or pulls us in. Negative features repel us, so while good performance can lead to a raise, poor performance can lead to losing a job.

Motivation can be a bit confusing because there's often a combination of push and pull on the internal and external sources, which cause us to act. To understand how motivation works, scientists consider a person's internal disposition as well as external factors. Your disposition is the internal desire to perform a particular action. In other words, disposition is an innate part of your personality, including your personal needs, wants, and desires. As I shared in my story earlier, my internal disposition is to learn. Learning, for me, is a natural, internal motivating driver. You may be aware of your predisposed motives. However, you may not be aware of a motivating driver that lies dormant within you until it's aroused or triggered.

For example, when you completed the Self-Awareness Assessment activity in Chapter 1, you may have been aware, for you, achievement is a motivating factor. So, you rated yourself high in that category. You feel good about yourself and satisfied when you complete a task or get a promotion at work. However, what may be lying dormant is your desire to feel empowered and in control. Perhaps you haven't recognized a need to feed your ego. Therefore, you may have scored yourself lower in the self-indulgence category. Regardless, once this psychological need was triggered by your achievement, another dormant psychological need emerged from the arousal process which occurred in your brain. This is what links your motivation and inspiration.

In conclusion, inspiration happens when the brain and mind are aroused, awakening a state of mind. You now realize you have underlying triggers in your conscious and unconscious mind that fire based on your internal desires and needs as well as external incentives and rewards. This knowledge will be important as we dive deeper into a discussion about how your brain and mind work together to determine internal motivation, a concept at the core of finding your personal superpowers for mastering self-motivation.

Since your personality is unique; you naturally have your own personal motives and values that incentivize or trigger your drive to satisfy your needs and desires. Self-Awareness Activity #2 will take you to the next step in discovering what motivates you.

ACTIVITY #2

WRITE YOUR AUTOBIOGRAPHY

Imagine you're living your best career/life!

Instructions: *Think about and respond to the following questions:*

1. **What is your vision for your life? Your vision is your purpose. It is your why.**
    a. Think about the life you want to live in 5, 10, 20, 30, 40, 50, 60, 70 years from now. What matters to you? Think about your health, relationships, spiritual walk, time, wealth, experiences, accomplishments, or contentment (being happy with who you are).
    b. Given the right circumstances, resources, and motivation what things could you accomplish?

2. **Describe in detail what it looks like:** ______________________________

____

____

____

3. **Describe how you feel:** ______________________________________

____

4. **In your best career/life as you've described it, what do you value most?**

____

____

5. **In your best career/life, what drivers, needs, or desires are being satisfied?**

____

____

6. **What is the title of your autobiographical documentary?**

____

____

KEY CONCEPTS

- ✓ Think of motivation as a journey which takes you from where you are, your current state, to where you desire to be, a future state.
- ✓ Motivation comes from the interactions among conscious and unconscious triggers linked to internal influencers such as desires and needs, and external factors such as incentives, rewards, and goals.
- ✓ Motivation involves biological, emotional, social, and cognitive forces that activate behavior. It is the *why* behind what drives human action.
- ✓ Inspiration is the awakening of a state of mind. Something touches you in such a way that it excites a desire within you to do something, whereas motivation is the process of moving to action. Inspiration is the creation of a motive which moves you to act.
- ✓ The field of cognitive behavior has demonstrated our behavior affects how we think and feel. How we think and feel affects our behavior. Inspiration is a pathway to change our way of thinking, feeling, and behaving.
- ✓ Motivation reflects something unique within each of us. It energizes us to gain what we value as desired outcomes like improved performance, personal growth, or a sense of purpose. Desires are personal, driven by our personality, talents, and disposition. However, fundamental drives, needs, and incentives are considered universal in our physical and psychological being.
- ✓ There are two groups of basic human needs: *physiological needs* and *psychological needs*. Physiological needs include food, water, and shelter. Psychological needs include affection, security, and self-esteem. Basic needs are considered *deficiency needs* because if they aren't met, we will strive to make up the deficiency. A third group of needs is referred to as *higher needs* or growth needs.
- ✓ *Drive* moves a person to satisfy a *need* or pursue an aspiration (*desire*).
- ✓ An *incentive* is an anticipated environmental feature such as

a reward or punishment that pulls an individual toward or away from something.

YOUR NOTES:

MOTIVATION IS WHY YOU DO THE THINGS YOU DO.

CHAPTER 3

How Motivation Works: It's All in Your Head

Why you do the things you do. What really drives your motivation? You may question how motivation works, but there's no question motivation is one of the most important factors to achieve success, however you define it. Whether you're an entrepreneur, an artist, a parent, leader, or simply a person who wants to do their best and contribute to a larger purpose, there's no underestimating the power of motivation.

All motivation comes from within, whether triggered by motives, desires, needs, or incentives. Motivation can be either extrinsic or intrinsic, meaning it's prompted by external incentives, arising from external factors or by internal motives, arising from internal factors. Extrinsic motivation happens when you engage in an activity due to an inner desire to achieve a reward or form of compensation. Intrinsic motivation is an inner desire to do something because you experience personal satisfaction and enjoy engaging in the activity.

Everyone is different; therefore, factors that motivate one person may not motivate another one. What some people see as externally or internally motivating may be different. For example, you may attend college because you enjoy learning new things, or you're interested in what you are learning, so you're intrinsically motivated. Conversely, others attend college to obtain a degree so they can enter a field that pays well and provides an opportunity to rise in status or wealth. Whether you're intrinsically or extrinsically motivated, the drive to engage springs from within. Understanding why you do the things you do will help you discover the motivational drivers within you and how to trigger them. This is another superpower!

Remember in Chapter 1, I stated you can activate a switch in your brain which allows you to be self-motivated. You have the extraordinary ability to determine and achieve optimal levels of performance as well as happiness through self-motivation. To learn how to turn on and off those switches in your brain, you need to learn basic information about how your brain functions. So, I'm going to take you on a brief guided tour of the biology of your brain. Heads up, this is the part of the book where we get into the science behind motivation!

WHAT DOES NEUROSCIENCE TELL US ABOUT MOTIVATION?

In recent years, the study of neuroscience, which means brain science, has progressed significantly due to breakthrough discoveries. Neuroscientists have determined our *state of mind* is rooted in this physical, electromagnetic, quantum, chemically based mass of tissue called the human brain. Furthermore, they've discovered the brain can turn on and off switches triggering the direction of your motivation. You'll find your superpower by learning to turn on and off the switches in your brain.

THE BIOLOGY AND FUNCTIONALITY OF THE BRAIN

The mysteries of our mind are many and complex. However, neuroscientists are unravelling some of these mysteries. Only a few decades ago scientists considered our brains to be a fixed, hardwired machine. More recently, we've learned as you think, you change the physical nature of your brain. In other words, your thoughts literally change the structure of your brain. So, what you think really impacts how you live your life. It is liberating to understand you aren't stuck with the brain you have, and you aren't a victim of your biology or circumstances.

The idea that our brains can change their structure and function through thought and activity is a revolutionary one. What's more exciting is you can apply this information to your personal and professional growth by kicking old habits and developing new ones. This breakthrough will empower you to develop your superpowers to get what you want out of your work and your life. This is great news!

Growing research is beginning to reveal how the brain and mind are both co-dependent and interrelated. The mind is where your flow of conscious and unconscious thought is generated. The brain is the core of your central nervous system where communication occurs to and from different areas of your body. Both the mind and the brain are shaped by two larger systems rooted in nature, the evolution of the brain, and nurture, which includes influencing factors like your environment and how you were raised. Because your mind and brain are co-dependent and interrelated, as your brain changes, your mind changes, and as your mind changes, your brain changes, sending signals to the rest of your body to act.

The study of the anatomy of the brain is known as neuroanatomy. The study of the brain's function is neuroscience. Neuroscience examines both the structure and function of the human brain and the nervous system. Neuroscientists use cellular and molecular biology, anatomy and physiology, human behavior and cognition, and other disciplines to map the brain at a mechanical level.

Neuro-networks

Your brain is a sophisticated network of functions. It's a complex and intricate information-processing mechanism, which controls every aspect of bodily and psychological functions. It's responsible for thought, creativity, emotions, intellect, memory, cognitive reasoning or common sense, social intelligence, sensory processing and interpretation, and intuition.

Most people unfortunately take their brains for granted. Scientists are just beginning to understand and talk about the superpowers in our brains related to learning and personal development. Only in the last decade or two have we truly contemplated how this three-pound mass, shaped like a head of cauliflower with a texture like tofu, has the ability to not only interpret the world, but to create it.

The human brain is made of 100 billion nerve cells called neurons. Neurons begin as round cell bodies which grow processes called axons and dendrites. Each nerve cell has one axon and as many as 100,000 dendrites. An adult brain contains well over 100,000 miles of axons and dendrites—enough to wrap around the earth more than four times. Dendrites contact other neurons through a specialized structure called synapses. Neurons communicate across synapses using chemical and electrical signals called neurotransmitters. This is the primary way neurons transmit information. It occurs through the creation of neuropathways and neural circuits that make up an elaborate network system. These neural pathways are strengthened through repetition and weakened when we don't reinforce those connections.

There are over two miles of neuronal network interconnections packed into every cubic millimeter of brain matter. In fact, in the average adult human brain, if you counted one each second, it would take more than three million years to finish. These connections are dynamic and in a constant state of change. This complex network of neural connections is continually adding, dropping, and changing its connections. They adapt and respond to how you experience the world around you. These connections guide our bodies, thoughts, emotions, and behaviors. Within these changing connections memories are stored, habits are learned, and personalities shaped, reinforcing certain patterns of brain activity and losing others.

In your brain, dopamine functions as a neurotransmitter, a chemical released by neurons to send signals to other nerve cells. The brain includes several distinct dopamine pathways, one of these plays a major role in the motivational part of reward-motivated behavior. The anticipation of most types of rewards increases the level of dopamine in your brain. This will become an important factor as we continue exploring how motivation works.

This may sound a bit heady, but I guarantee understanding how the brain works will become relevant as I unpack the concept of self-motivation. I believe, for you to change your brain, you must believe it is possible to do so, and not just take someone else's word for it. So, stay with me.

Hippocrates, the father of Western medicine, recognized centuries ago, "Men should know that from nothing else, but the brain come joys, delights, laughter, and jests and sorrows, grief, despondency, and lamentations."

More recently, Francis Crick, a major biologist of our time echoed a similar idea: "You, your joys and your sorrows, your memories and your ambition, your sense of personal identity and free will, are in fact no more than the behavior of a vast assembly of nerve cells and their associated molecules." In addition, the brain is also responsible for how we perceive our world and how we behave within it. So, understanding how your brain works is understanding yourself.

NEUROPLASTICITY AND NEUROGENESIS

By now, you've discovered your brain is a dynamic ecosystem of neurons and networks. Let's dig a little deeper.

Previously, scientists believed brain development only occurred during childhood and adolescence. It was widely believed once we reached adulthood, our brain was basically hardwired. It was fixed and static, and, unfortunately, by your early twenties, you were stuck with what you had. However, in the last generation significant breakthroughs in neuroscience have occurred. Scientists have learned our brains are plastic; meaning, they're malleable throughout our lifetime. Thanks to new discoveries in neuroscience, we know much more about how the brain works and how *neuroplasticity* enables us to literally rewire parts of our brains. We can retrain our brain regarding how we connect our thoughts, images, words, and behaviors to adapt to how we experience the world.

Neuroplasticity, also referred to as brain plasticity, is a relatively new term describing the brain's ability to reorganize itself and form new neural connections throughout life. It's defined as our nervous system's ability to change its activity in response to intrinsic or extrinsic stimuli by reorganizing its structure, functions, or connections. This process enables the brain to adapt, reorganize, and recover from insult or injury to the brain body. The exciting news is, your human brain is designed to learn, develop, and heal throughout your life.

Neuroplasticity is the process where memory materializes, learning occurs, and experiences are chronicled. When you make connections between ideas and images, your neurons fire and encode those ideas and images to memory. You may have heard the phrase, "Cells that fire together wire together." When neurons fire together, they create a neural pathway. The more often they fire together, the stronger that pathway grows. The more prolonged the excitation between cells, the stronger the connection. As a result, the more likely they are to fire together in the future.

As the firing between your neurons continue, the genes within those neurons are turned on to construct more building blocks for the neural pathway infrastructure. This is how you activate or turn on that switch I referred to in your brain. This is also how habits are established. The more frequently you say, do, and think certain words, behaviors, and thoughts, the stronger the pathway becomes and the easier, quicker, and more comfortable it becomes to stick to new habits.

Think about the last time you started a new job. At first, it felt like putting on a new pair of shoes. The shoes may be a bit uncomfortable initially, but once you break them in, they become your go-to shoes. When starting a new job, you don't know where the supplies are. You're not sure how to access various computer programs you're required to use, you're learning how to interact with your boss and co-workers, and you're doing your best to assimilate into the culture of the company and adjust to a new daily work routine.

During this time of onboarding, you're making conscious decisions regarding your thoughts, emotions, and behaviors. These decisions are of your choosing. They'll determine how you act as you assimilate into your new work environment and learn the tasks required by your job. During this process, your unconscious and conscious mind is working with your brain to establish and strengthen neuropathways that guide your thoughts, emotions, and behaviors. Over time, you learn the routine of the office, the culture of the company, and the nuances of relationships with your boss and co-workers. It all begins to feel more and more like a comfortable, well-worn pair of shoes.

This is an example of how your mind and brain are co-dependent and interrelated. It also exemplifies the process I described earlier in this chapter, as your brain changes, your mind changes, and as your mind changes, your brain changes, sending signals to the rest of your body to act. Hopefully, you aren't breaking in new shoes at the same time you're starting a new job.

The opposite is true as well, "Neurons that fire apart, wire apart." In other words, if you don't use it, you'll lose it. When you stop speaking, thinking, and behaving in certain ways, those neural pathways will weaken and no longer be your quick, easy, comfortable default. This is how you disable or turn off a switch in your brain and break a habit. As you know, breaking habits can be challenging; however, the longer those neurons are not firing the less likely you are to fall back to previous habits or thought patterns.

Neurogenesis is the process where neurons are formed in the brain. As I mentioned above, neuroscientists until recently believed our central nervous system, including the brain, was incapable of generating new cells once we become adults. However, recent research reveals neural stem cells can produce new cells. As a result of stem cell research, neuroscientists discovered our brain cells can divide indefinitely, producing more cells. Because neuroscientists have discovered cells can divide and differentiate into many types of cells, neurogenesis, or the process of new brain cell generation, is now widely accepted as a normal process that occurs in a healthy adult brain.

Why is this important?

Remember when your parents said, if you drink alcohol, you kill off thousands of brain cells? We have a finite number of brain cells so we can't afford to kill them off. Well, your parents were well-intentioned when they lectured you. They wanted to protect you from the ill-effects of partying too hard or too much. In their defense, they told the truth, or at least what they believed was the truth. However, even though alcohol can destroy precious brain cells, most likely, you won't be brain dead by the time you grow out of your partying phase of life, if you drink responsibly. The good news is scientists have learned we can create entirely new, elaborate connections with new brain cells and boost or strengthen existing neural connections up to the point we take our last breath.

Your brain is constantly being shaped and reshaped, transforming yourself based on how you experience life and the world around you. So, the key discovery is how you frame your life experience is how you experience your life. By changing your perception of your experience, you can change how you actually experience the experience.

Knowing your brain can change by rewiring its hardwire as well as understanding it can generate new brain cells, will be essential later when I explore how you can change the way you think and behave by how you think and behave. That may sound like double talk, but I promise it will make sense when you get to Chapter 4, *Mastering Your Mindset*. I simply ask you to keep an open mind, be fully present, and believe in yourself.

The good news is you're more than halfway through our tour of the inner workings of your brain. Stick with me, okay?

Our brains are complex with many moving parts and layers, so I will take a few short cuts discussing the general road map about how it functions. My goal isn't to make you a neuroscientist but to give you a glimpse into a few more relevant aspects about how it works with your mind. Basically, your brain works with two systems, the sympathetic and parasympathetic.

- The *sympathetic* is activated when the brain is called on to stimulate your stress triggered fight or flight response, which affects your emotions, thinking, and reasoning.
- The *parasympathetic* nervous system inhibits your body from overworking and restores it to a calm and composed state.

The brain is set up to naturally ensure survival, this is your nature-based brain. However, it's also designed to be flexible so you can grow, learn, and create.

Remember the discussions about neuroplasticity and neurogenesis. Your individual development, as a unique person, is nurture-based.

THE KEY PARTS OF THE BRAIN RELEVANT TO DEVELOPING YOUR SUPERPOWERS

Although your entire brain is serving you all the time, specific areas of the brain serve you in different capacities.

- The *Prefrontal Cortex* is often referred to as the executive functioning part of the brain. This is where reasoning and much of our cognitive, analytical thinking occurs. It's also responsible for conscious language of thought, verbal expression, and self-awareness. The prefrontal cortex plays a role in planning and motivating action as well. The prefrontal cortex is a significant relay in the reward circuit and is modulated by dopamine.
- The *Frontal Lobe* is the area of the brain responsible for focus, spontaneity, language, judgement, motor function, impulse control, and social and sexual behavior.
- The *Parietal Lobe* located near the center of the brain is the area where our orientation of space and time is located. It's also where we find our primary sensory area. It's where impulses from the skin such as warmth, cold, pain, and touch are interpreted.
- The *Nucleus Accumbens,* part of the basal ganglia, is located midbrain. It plays a central role in the reward circuit. Its operation is based chiefly on two essential neurotransmitters: dopamine, which promotes desire, and serotonin, whose effects include satiety and inhibition. It also plays a role in addiction.
- The *Limbic System* is often referred to as the emotional center of the brain. It is the area of the brain associated with the language of emotions, feeling tones, and implicit memory. It is the part of the brain that feels and reacts. Located at the top of the brainstem and buried under the cortex, it's generally under control of the "thinking part" of the brain. It can react to stimuli on its own such as the fight, flight, and freeze responses to stress or threats.

For example, when a person is in danger and must respond quickly, as an act of self-preservation, the limbic system is aroused, preparing them for action, initiating a release of chemicals throughout the body. When you watch a shocking news story or receive an upsetting message, like criticism from others, the limbic system is stimulated. Chemicals are released as if you're being attacked, and they activate the fear and stress emotions and related hormones.

When threats are detected, messages are sent by the limbic system triggering the release of epinephrine, adrenaline and norepinephrine, or noradrenaline into the bloodstream. These in turn trigger a series of responses from your organs and muscles throughout the body as well as cortisol. *Cortisol* is often called the "stress hormone" because of its connection to your stress response. It increases heartrate, blood pressure, and respiration while shutting down the systems that are unnecessary like digestion and reproduction. Simultaneously, dopamine, which is the neurotransmitter known as the happy or pleasure hormone that fires when you anticipate reward or receive an unexpected reward or praise, can be negatively affected when you feel threatened.

Before leaving our conversation about the brain, I also want to discuss the amygdala, hippocampus, thalamus, and hypothalamus. Each of these areas play an important role in how motivation is originated in the brain.

The amygdala is located within the limbic system and is involved with feeling and discerning emotion, especially fear. The amygdala is most stimulated by survival situations, those involving danger, as well as events which survival depends, like those that warn of danger or distress, as well as events that indicate essential needs like food and water.

Your fight, flight, or freeze response is called "hyperarousal" and it's the built-in self-preservation mechanism made up of a series of neuro, chemical, and hormonal processes which prepare your body to effectively respond to threats by fighting, fleeing, or freezing. The brain is hardwired to react to certain threatening stimuli.

- The sympathetic response to threats is a feeling of temporary acute stress.
- The parasympathetic function eventually returns the body to a normal state of *homeostasis*.

If you ever had a job interview, given an important speech or presentation, or were talked into doing a bungee jump, chances are you've experienced the physiological reactions to acute stress. Your heart was racing, your breathing increased, your palms began to sweat, and in some cases, you rushed to the bathroom.

These physical symptoms are involuntary, instinctive, and hard to suppress.

Another important function of the amygdala is the consolidation of memory and emotion. This combination is seen most famously in Pavlov's experiments of *classical conditioning* and *fear conditioning*, where the subject remembers and reacts to stimuli, whether it's positive, neutral, or negative.

The hippocampus, thalamus, and hypothalamus are located within your limbic system and involve the operation of memory consolidation and emotional regulation. Studies reveal that when an emotion such as reward or pain is associated with a behavior, it is encoded and stored in memory. This part of the brain also contributes to hormone management.

Let's put some of these ideas in context.

When Mandi sits at her desk to begin her workday, she is triggered by a desire to see what's happening on her social media feed. She chooses to either scroll or not to scroll her feed. Her choice is based on the value she puts on the consequences of her actions. She evaluates the anticipated and immediate rewards she will feel when she

- satisfies her short-term curiosity by looking at her feed before working,
- contrasted with the delayed potential positive consequences that may come by completing work,
- or the negative potential consequences, including stress if she doesn't finish her work on time.
- In that moment, the parietal lobe engages, she
- activates the key parts of her brain,
- analyzes and prioritizes utilizing the prefrontal cortex,
- decides to control or not control her impulse to look at her feed using the frontal lobe,
- considers the reward associated with the release of feel-good dopamine or cortisol triggered by the nucleus accumbens as well as the limbic system. The release of these hormones causes positive or negative feelings.

Are you wondering why I'm explaining all this? The brain is arguably the most important organ in our human body. It controls and coordinates actions and reactions, allowing us to think, feel, and act. It also enables us to have memories and feelings—the things that make us human. By understanding how your brain and your mind work, you'll discover you have more control over how to use the combined power of your conscious and unconscious mind to think and behave in a more flexible, persistent, resilient, and self-motivated way.

Trust me, science now backs up the notion that you can train your brain.

BUILDING A NEW NEUROPATHWAY

Building a new neuropathway involves three basic stages:

STAGE 1: *Stimulus*: A stimulus activates receptors in the brain and excites neurons. Whether the stimulus is generated from an intrinsic or extrinsic factor, it triggers a desire or need, which, in turn, motivates a response. Stimuli can come from sight, sound, smell, taste, touch, or even pain.

STAGE 2: *Response*: Your response is the behavior you choose to engage. Behavior is dependent on how you choose to think or act based on the stimulus.

STAGE 3: *Reinforcement*: Reinforcement occurs through repetition, which is dependent on the reward that activates a release of dopamine and other feel-good hormones. The intensity and frequency of reinforcement is associated with the value you place on the reward.

In this activity, I'll break down the process to create new neuropathways. By following the steps outlined below, you can practice the process. You'll build upon what I've discussed in Chapters 1, 2, and 3. As you go through the steps, think about the parts of the brain you're engaging. It may help to revisit the self-awareness activities you completed in Chapters 1 and 2.

- **Chapter 1**: Review what naturally energizes you such as *achievement, personal success, mastery, self-indulgence, purpose, relatedness, avoidance*, or maybe you've identified another *intrinsic* motivating factor.
- **Chapter 2:** Review your *best career or life* as you've described it. How will you *feel* living your best life, what you *value*, and what *desires* or *needs* you declared?

ACTIVITY #3

STEPS TO CREATING A NEW NEUROPATHWAY

STAGE 1: STIMULUS

STEP 1: Establish a goal you want to achieve. It may be a long-term or short-term goal, or somewhere in between. Use the SMART goal guide.

S = Specificity: Be specific in describing your goal.

M = Measurable: Think about how you will know you have achieved your goal in terms of measuring your achievement.

A = Attainable: Be sure your goal is attainable and realistic. It is okay if it may take a long time and have many moving parts.

R = Relevant: Think of your goal in terms of what makes you happy, where your talents and passion fit in, and does it drive a motivational factor for you.

T = Timebound: Finally, give yourself a timetable when you expect to see results. Keep in mind, you can always adjust your timetable based on the reality of your progress, resources, and desire to achieve your goal.

By setting a new goal you engage the thinking and feeling parts of your brain by identifying a gap in what you have and what you need or want. Sometimes we set goals in terms of what we don't want rather than what we do want. What do you truly want? For example, if you set a goal to spend less time with social media – maybe your true goal is to manage your time better so you can get a promotion at work.

STEP 2: Identify a behavior you want to start, stop, or continue to move you toward achieving your goal. To begin, select a simple behavior you'd like to change.

Doing this step activates your cognitive thinking in the prefrontal lobe: satisfying a need or want; or, anticipating a reward either intrinsic or extrinsic.

STEP 3: Think about and describe how you'll feel when you successfully change this behavior.

Step 3 engages your emotional connection found in the limbic system, activating feel good hormones or avoiding the release of stress hormones.

STEP 4: On a scale of 1-10 assign a value to what meaning or level of importance this behavior has in your effort to achieve your goal. Consider how this change will move you closer to achieving your goal.

This activates the pre-frontal cortex, the executive function and many other regions of the brain related to relevance and desire which drives your natural tendencies to learn.

STEP 5: Create a trigger.

Your mind is active, continuously looking for cues, which it responds to in anticipation of satisfying a need or want. These cues excite neurons. Creating a trigger can be as simple as writing yourself a note reminding you to be aware of something or take an action.

STEP 6: Think how the change you've identified will satisfy your need or want.

This thought process, which springs from the nucleus accumbens and limbic system internalizes your motive, making it intrinsic as well as triggering the release of dopamine, since there is an anticipated reward.

STAGE 2: RESPONSE

STEP 1: Make a conscious choice to act.

The executive functions of the brain discussed earlier can change the way you think and behave by changing the way you think and behave.

STEP 2: Act

Taking action activates the chemicals in your brain that build or reinforce neuropathways such as neurons, synapses, and neurotransmitters. Neuroplasticity is occurring—remember, "cells that fire together wire together."

STAGE 3: REINFORCEMENT

STEP 1: Establish a reward. The reward can be simply self-talk acknowledging your success, an internal high-five, or you can establish an external reward or incentive. Decide upon your reward in advance.

Establishing a reward trains your brain to recognize which actions are worth your effort and remember it for the future. Over time, reinforcement establishes an automatic default behavior or new habit. Reinforcement helps to develops stronger neuropathways and form memory.

MY EXAMPLE

My internal *motivating factor* is learning and teaching.

My *desire* is to write a book I can use to help readers and others become more self-motivated.

Living my *best life and career* involves training, speaking, and coaching emerging leaders and professionals how to discover their personal superpowers to master self-motivation.

My *goal* is to write a book on self-motivation. I've dreamed of doing this and feel it's my life *purpose*.

Therefore, I put a *value* of 10 on its importance. As I *see* myself facilitating a seminar, I'll be in my zone. This will bring a natural high for me. I'll *feel* exhilarated.

The *behavior I want to change* is to stop procrastinating. Too often, I let distractions take over my time, self-sabotaging my progress.

I established a visual *trigger*. I created and displayed a mock-up design of my book cover including the title and tagline. Now, every time I sit down at my computer, I'm reminded of my goal, my *want* in accomplishing the goal, and the *need* to work for at least an hour on the book every day.

My *reward* is to use my read aloud audio feature on my computer to hear my progress, even though I know I may need to go back and make changes. I feel good about making progress. That's my reward. I finish my time working on the book with a thought or sentence I've started but not yet finished. This *trigger* reminds me where I left off and that I'm still in the process.

After doing this for several weeks, I rarely look at my mock book cover design. I *jump into the writing process* with *focused energy*. By creating this positive *neuropathway* and *reinforcing* it as a habit, I'm *sustaining my motivation* and am well on my way to finishing the book!

RECAP

Stimuli trigger behaviors that satisfy a need or want. This is reinforced by a reward. This cycle when repeated, builds and strengthens new neuropathways, establishing a new way of thinking and behaving.

KEY CONCEPTS

- ✓ All motivation comes from within, whether triggered by motives, desires, needs, or incentives. Motivation can be extrinsic or intrinsic, which means it's prompted by
    - external incentives, arising from external factors or
    - internal motives, arising from internal factors.
- ✓ Neuroscientists have determined our state of mind is rooted in this physical, electromagnetic, quantum, chemically based mass called the human brain. Additionally, they've discovered the brain can turn on and off switches, which trigger the direction of your motivation. You'll find your superpowers by learning how to turn on and off these switches in your brain.
- ✓ Neuroscientists have discovered you can change the physical nature of your brain. In other words, your thoughts change the structure of your brain, so what you think affects how you live your life.
- ✓ Neuro networks guide your body, thoughts, emotions, and behaviors. These changing connections are where memories are stored, habits learned, and personality shaped by reinforcing certain patterns of brain activity and losing others.
- ✓ Neuroplasticity is the process where memory materializes, learning occurs, and experiences are chronicled. When you make connections between ideas and images, your neurons are firing and encoding those ideas and images into memory.
- ✓ Your entire brain is serving you all the time. However, specific areas of the brain serve us in different capacities.
- ✓ Understanding how the brain and mind work, you'll discover you have more control over how to use the combined power of your conscious and unconscious mind to think and behave in a more flexible, persistent, resilient, and self-motivated way.

YOUR NOTES:

MOTIVATION IS A STATE OF MIND

CHAPTER 4

Motivation Psychology: Mastering Your Mindset

Oprah Winfrey was born into poverty but has famously become one of the world's wealthiest and most influential women. Oprah is a huge believer and supporter of positive mindset. Her philosophy includes:

- taking control of your life,
- making the best of each moment because it prepares you for your next moment, and
- your individual choices and thoughts are central to living your dreams.

She lives by the words, "Everything in your world is created by what you think." Also, "With every experience, you alone are painting your own canvas, thought by thought, choice by choice." Winfrey's philosophy is a way of thinking that manifests itself in a way of behaving. A mindset can arise out of a world view or philosophy of life.

Before he became a world-renowned comedian and actor, Jim Carrey was struggling. In 1985, he wrote himself a check for 10 million dollars for "acting services rendered." He dated it for ten years in the future and kept it in his wallet. Fast forward ten years. In 1995, Carrey was cast in the movie "Dumb and Dumber," for you guessed it -- 10 million dollars. He claims this wasn't a mere coincidence or good luck. During a 1997 television interview, Carrey explained his motivation as more than just visualizing success. He knew he had to work hard and stay focused on his goal. Carrey said, "You can't just visualize and then, you know, go eat a sandwich." He visualized himself as a successful actor, set his intention, believed he could succeed, developed a persistent positive mindset, and worked hard.

The world's most famous surfer today might be Bethany Hamilton. One of the most inspirational comeback stories of our era, Bethany turned trauma into an incredible story of triumph. At the tender age of seven, Bethany was already surfing the pipelines off the Hawaiian shores. At eight years old, Bethany won her first of many amateur championship titles, winning first place in Hawaii's Rell Sunn Menehune competition. At age 13, this young champion was making headlines, not only for her accomplishments as a surfer, but her extraordinary comeback after being attacked by a 14-foot-long shark.

Bethany lost 60 percent of her blood in the attack and lost her left arm almost up to her shoulder. Despite the massive injury, Bethany possessed the mindset of a champion. She refused to let the setback define her career or deter her passion for surfing. She not only won more top surfing competitions, but her experience led to a book, a documentary, a feature film, "Soul Surfer," and many television appearances, including a third-place finish on "The Amazing Race" in 2014. Hamilton's positive attitude, determination, and faith continues to touch and inspire lives around the world.

Becoming a billionaire before age 30, co-founder of Facebook, Dustin Moskovitz believed by being mindful and aware of his mental and physical state, he could guide his actions and thoughts with intention. He shared his philosophy and mindset in an interview with Fast Company in 2014 when he said, "Mindfulness has helped me succeed in almost every dimension of life. By stopping regularly to look inward and become aware of my mental state, I stay connected to the source of my actions and thoughts and can guide them with considerably more intention." This is also a philosophy he now encourages at Asana, an organizational software company he co-owns. He disclosed,

"By bringing full presence to each interaction, I am able to avoid missteps and stay focused on my real purpose for every conversation. This guides both my personal and work life: we apply this principle at Asana by making sure there are regular forums and opportunities for reflection, from periodic peer feedback and self-reviews to punctuated episodes of work, in between which we re-evaluate every part of the company."

According to the September 2020 issue of Forbes, Asana's valuation was $5 billion. Moskovitz' life's philosophy is not only his personal mindset, but the culture in which his company operates. In each of these stories, we see how people create personal, professional, and organizational success with a unique combination of skills, mindset, and motivation.

There's no shortage of inspiring stories from people who've succeeded in accomplishing their dreams. Success stories provide evidence the mind is a powerful means to achieve your goals. Largely a matter of choice, your mindset determines your interpretations and responses to your personal experiences as well as your perception of the world. How you choose your mindset shapes your relationship with yourself, others, and your world view, so choose wisely.

Deepening our understanding of how and why we behave the way we do helps us gain insight into our mindset. First, let's start with a few basics and explore the science behind the study of mindset. Then we'll move into how you too can master your mindset. Things to know:

- *Psychology* is the study of mind and behavior. It encompasses biological factors and environmental influences such as social, cultural, and personal experiences that affect how people think, act, and feel.
- *Motivation Psychology* is the science behind what drives us to achieve goals and behave in particular ways. It includes the biology of the brain, human thought, development, personality, emotion, motivation, and behavior.
- *Motivational Science* is a behavioral science that studies what elements make up human motivation and how motivational processes work.
- *Self-motivation* is the autonomy to be a causal agent in your own life.
- *Mindset* is a frame of mind. Your mindset is unique to you. It's the personal perspective or lens through which you observe yourself and the world. Mindset is shaped by beliefs, assumptions, and thoughts. These are affected by your personality, which is your natural disposition and environmental factors, including how you were raised, experiences during your formative years, religion, social and cultural influences, and education. Your mindset determines your interpretation of the world around you and thus, how you approach life. Most importantly, the sciences of psychology, neuroscience, and motivation agree, your mindset is malleable.

Pulling all this together helps us understand how motivation is sustained. It's sustained by your state of mind. Knowing you can retrain your brain and change your mindset empowers you to be a causal agent in your own life.

MASTERING YOUR MINDSET

"The mind is everything. What you think, you become," — Buddha.

We have discovered mindset is created by how you *view* your experience: it *shapes* your world; it's a developed *habit*; and, most significantly, it's malleable. Through discoveries in neuroscience, specifically in neuroplasticity, researchers have learned you can change your mind by changing your thoughts.

To master your mindset, start by being aware of your current state of mind. Become cognizant of your beliefs, assumptions, and thoughts. As you read through the next section of this chapter, reflect on the thoughts you're currently thinking. Ask yourself, are your current beliefs, assumptions, and thoughts serving you in becoming the person you want to be? If not, then you can change them. As we've seen with the examples of famous people like Tiger Woods, Joy Mangano, Oprah Winfrey, Jim Carrey, Bethany Hamilton, and Dustin Moskovitz, to achieve your full potential, your thoughts need to be an exact reflection of who you want to be and the life you want to live.

Are you ready to master your mindset? Let's get started.

Perception and Framing

Perception is your sensory experience of the world. It involves recognizing environmental stimuli and prompts behaviors in response to these stimuli. Perception encompasses your physical senses: touch, sight, sound, smell, and taste, as well as your sixth sense, intuition. Intuition or instinct is your gut feeling about a situation and inclination toward a particular response. It gives you the ability to *feel* as if you know something is real without relying entirely on cognitive reasoning. Your sixth sense bridges the gap between the conscious and unconscious parts of your mind using both your gut feeling and reasoning. The conscious mind is masterful in taking what you touch, see, hear, smell, and taste and assigning logic to the stimuli to create a physical and emotional response. When you tap into your intuition or sixth sense, the unconscious mind searches the past, present, and potential future experiences to assign beliefs, assumptions, and thoughts that frame your experience.

Here's an example of how you can use your perception to frame an experience:

It's late and the mall is closing. As you exit through the heavy glass doors, you survey the parking lot. It's quiet, dark, and devoid of both cars and people. Your conscious mind quickly works with your unconscious mind to frame the situation as potentially dangerous. You may experience anxiousness or downright fear. The reasoning part of your brain says, based on past, present, and potential future experiences, assumptions, and beliefs someone could approach you and do harm. So, your cognitive reasoning along with your instinct to protect yourself sets up a response to have your keys in hand and your finger on the panic button as you hurry to your car.

Another person might perceive this situation in a different way. Based on their beliefs, assumptions, and thoughts, they may frame this as a welcome quiet stroll to their car after a hectic afternoon of shopping. They take the opportunity to feel the gentle breeze of the night and take a deep breath of fresh air after being in the staleness of the stores. They feel joyful in the peacefulness of the moment. How we view our experience determines how we experience the experience.

Open-mindedness

Swiss psychologist and genetic epistemologist, Jean Piaget, known for his research in early childhood development, suggested as children we naturally sort knowledge through our experiences and interactions into groupings known as schemas. *Schemas* are cognitive frameworks which help us interpret information and organize it in categories. Piaget suggested when new information is gained,

- it can be easily *assimilated* into existing schemas,
- *accommodated* by revising an existing schema, or in some cases,
- a new category of information is created, known as accommodation.

Assimilation is the process of making new information fit your current understanding of the world. When assimilating new information, we tend to modify our experiences so we can incorporate them into our existing ideas. Assimilating schemas often contribute to stereotyping or close-mindedness. The process of accommodation advances learning. It lets you change your existing ideas and become open and receptive to new ones, contributing to open-mindedness. Assimilation and accommodation don't happen only in childhood development. Cognitive therapists find adults process information the same way.

Why is it important to understand the concept of assimilating and accommodating in the context of developing an open mind?

Open-mindedness means being receptive to new information, ideas, and ways in which you view the world. Being open to other ways of thinking springs from an awareness of your thoughts and being open to accommodating or creating new schemas, hence reframing your perspective.

Open-mindedness is generally considered an important and valuable attribute in management and other team settings. Open-minded people are more inclined to listen and seriously consider alternative viewpoints. There is much to gain in your professional and personal life from opening the door to your mind, letting new ideas and beliefs enter. When you do, you free yourself from the limits of existing beliefs, assumptions, and thoughts. This isn't to suggest all your existing beliefs, assumptions, and thoughts should be discarded. An open mind simply provides a platform on which you can build ideas, learn new things, and shift your perspective to develop a positive, optimistic mindset.

MINDSETS THAT SHAPE OUR WORLD

Your mindset works in an interpretive way and is shaped by your internal monologue, your self-talk. This internal monologue evaluates and judges every observation and piece of information as evidence that either supports or doesn't support your beliefs about yourself, others, or the world. It affects the outcomes in your life in two possible ways. Your monologue either limits or liberates your potential. Let's consider a few of the major types of mindset.

Growth versus Fixed Mindset

Dr. Carol Dweck, one of the world's leading researchers on the topic of mindset, has spent decades studying achievement and success to understand why some people thrive in the face of obstacles and why others retreat. She's found people with a growth mindset are more successful than those with a fixed mindset. A fixed mindset is the belief your abilities are fixed traits that cannot change. Furthermore, people with a fixed mindset believe talent, intelligence, and circumstances alone lead to success. Any failure validates their lack of intelligence and opportunity. Their limited abilities prevent them from achieving their goals. They're constrained by limiting beliefs and thoughts. Examples of limiting beliefs and thoughts might include:

- I am not good with technology and computers.
- I am not worthy of living in a big, beautiful house.
- I am not strategic or clever enough to be a business owner.
- It's hard for me to come up with solutions to problems.
- I was born in poverty; therefore, I will never have the opportunity to realize my dreams.

A fixed mindset will ensure you have a difficult time staying motivated and accomplishing your goals. It will result in missing out on experiences and opportunities to avoid the possibility of failure. Ironically, failure and making mistakes help us grow and improve.

A growth mindset, on the other hand, is the notion your intelligence and abilities grow with time, experience, and effort. It doesn't evaluate or judge. Instead, it's curious, open-minded, and has an appetite for exploration and discovery. People with a growth mindset welcome learning and seek information to form new strategies. They're open to inspiration. They embrace problems and challenges as opportunities to develop new skills and grow.

Positive versus Negative Mindset

Scientific research reveals how important embracing positive emotions and adaptive behaviors are to living a satisfying, productive life. Recent studies show people who experience and express positive attitudes are more likely to be satisfied with their life. They are productive and satisfied at work, and they enjoy more rewarding relationships. As a result, they're more likely to reach their desired goals. Additionally, people who experience and express positivity are more likely to be physically healthier and may even live longer.

Positive psychologists have noted a combination of three elements which contribute to living "the good life." The good life being defined by a sense of contentment and flourishing. Those elements are *positive relationships with others, positive individual traits and virtues* (disposition), and *life regulation qualities*. The good news is a positive mindset can be cultivated through your thoughts and actions. Positive relationships are the outcome of love, forgiveness, altruistic concerns and behavior, and a sense of connection which links to one's purpose and meaning. Positive traits include the ability to play, be creative and curious, and virtues include integrity, courage, and humility. Finally, life regulation qualities include how you manage your emotions (emotional intelligence), frame your experiences, and interact with others.

Several studies in psychology have demonstrated being positive and open-minded enhances your creativity, broadens your experiences by opening your mind to try new things, pushes the boundaries of your comfort zone, and enables you to see things from a different perspective. In contrast, negativity reduces your willingness to try new things, narrows your vision for possibilities, and constricts thinking. Negativity is often fueled by your inner critic or monologue, and results in negative moods and emotions. A negative mindset can amplify your negative feelings and make you feel stuck in ruminating and pondering everything. Rumination is dwelling in sadness, rehashing bad experiences or memories. It's listening to limiting beliefs and negative self-talk like, "You can't do this!" Or, "You're not good enough, smart enough, talented enough, etc."

Negative moods and emotions contribute to an increase in anxiety and stress. Negative people are less creative, productive, and have greater difficulty developing and maintaining connections and relationships with others. When negativity spins out of control, it's possible to find yourself in a downward spiral of dysfunction and even depression.

Victim versus Accountable Mindset

People in a victim mindset tend to ruminate in self-pity. People in a victim mindset are more likely to be reactive versus proactive. Reactive people believe they aren't responsible for what they say and do. Instead, they blame others for their circumstances and outcomes. They spend time and energy complaining about things rather than doing something about a situation. They are prone to procrastinate, thereby avoiding their situation. They are less willing to take risks to resolve issues. These individuals would rather engage in negative or reactive behaviors than face up to and accept their circumstances, then take the steps necessary to move forward.

People with an accountability mindset believe they can manage their career and life. They're proactive about controlling their thoughts and actions. They don't waste time or energy dwelling in "woe is me" internal dialogues. Instead, they focus on what they can manage and move forward.

Clearly, mindset plays a critical role in our day-to-day lives. Your state of mind is linked to happiness and success. It's the lens that filters how you see yourself and the world. You have a choice to view your environment as an opportunity, which supports your goals or as an obstacle that thwarts your effort to achieve your goals. It can be full of distractions that result in procrastination or avoidance, or positive challenges that help you grow and flourish.

It's one thing to be motivated by inspiration and another to sustain your motivation and go the distance. Sustained motivation is linked to your beliefs, assumptions, and thoughts, which you can change at any time. That doesn't mean it will be easy. This is a superpower. Once you start mastering your mindset, life will become easier and a lot more enjoyable.

Shifting your mindset requires retraining your brain. Creating new neuropathways takes intentional effort to change how you think and behave. The steps outlined in Activity #4 will be your guide to changing your mindset.

ACTIVITY #4

MASTERING YOUR MINDSET

Review and reflect on the three steps: Awareness, Acceptance, and Action.

Awareness: *Becoming an observer is a critical skill in mastering your mindset. Observing yourself requires an awareness of your beliefs, assumptions, and thoughts. It also means you're mindful of your emotions, impulses, and behaviors. This is challenging since many emotions, impulses, and behaviors are automatic reactions based on how your brain is wired. This is largely due to the neuropathways discussed in Chapter 3 that have been strengthened from sustained habits. To change your brain, you must put forth the effort to break old habits and create new ones. Reflect on the following:*

- Become aware of your mindset. Are you falling into the trap of a fixed, negative, or victim mindset?
- Be aware of the inner critic or negative self-talk that may dominate your internal dialogue.
- Reflect on your beliefs. Do they limit or liberate you?
- Be aware of the language you use. Do you use negative words or positive ones? Do you use empowering statements such as "I can" or "I will" versus disempowering statements such as "I can't" or "I don't know how?"
- Pay attention to your inner circle. Do you surround yourself with people who are accepting, open-minded, and optimistic, or are they toxic, constantly complaining, or whining about their life and circumstances? You may need to change your inner circle. If that's impossible, be aware their mindset and toxic language doesn't need to be yours. Focus on people who energize you and avoid those who are energy vampires, sucking you dry.
- Be aware of your own energy. If your energy is positive, you'll attract others with positive energy. When you complain and blame, there's never a shortage of people who want to jump on the misery wagon with you.
- Pay attention to your triggers. When you recognize what triggers an emotional reaction within, you can regulate your response in a more

controlled, positive manner. When you start recognizing your triggers, you can observe your impulses and avoid acting on them. As you retrain your brain, you'll consciously create new patterns and behaviors, which over time, will become your new automatic response.

Acceptance: *Practicing acceptance isn't a sign of weakness or defeat; it is a starting point for change. Accepting where you are prepares you for the future, allowing yourself to meet yourself where you are. Acceptance is a choice. It may be difficult to face the truth and knowing you must push forward, dedicating time, energy, and other resources to accomplish your goals. Finally, accept that you aren't broken, you're simply willing to improve and enhance your life. Consider the following:*

- Accept your beliefs, assumptions, and thoughts may need to change.
- Pause and think about the lens in which you use to see yourself, your situation, others, or the world. What mindsets don't serve you? Acknowledge your unhelpful thoughts and push them aside. The more you're rooted in negativity, the stronger those neuropathways become. Whereas, the more you embrace a positive mindset, the stronger those neuropathways become. Eventually, positivity will become a natural, comfortable space where you live. Consider the person you want to be and dwell on the mindset that will help you arrive.
- Be open to learning and growing. This means stretch your comfort zone. The only way you grow and succeed to accomplish your goals is by challenging yourself, which may include challenging your mindset. Our minds are like a muscle. Developing mental strength requires exercise for your mind. Reinforce your progress by continuing the practice of your new mindset.
- You're a magnificent creation with a mind, body, and spirit that is uniquely yours.

Action: *Acting pushes you to expand your comfort zone, which helps you create new ways of thinking and behaving. When you act differently, you create positive change based on new patterns of thought and behavior. Repeated actions create habits. Change and success are an ongoing process; your actions and habits will lead you to live the life you imagine. Consider the following:*

- Establish your goals. Your goals should make sense to you. They should be expressed in specific, measurable terms. They should be attainable. Break lofty goals down into smaller goals, so they feel more realistic. Your goals must be meaningful and have purpose to you or they'll become less important and relevant. Finally, establish timelines about when you want to achieve both your smaller goals and your ultimate goal.
- Turn your limiting mindset into a liberating one by replacing your perception and reality filters.
    - Open your mind and reframe your perspective
    - Be willing to explore, be curious, and be creative
- Develop new habits by using triggers, reminders, and repetition. We will discuss more about developing habits throughout the next chapters.
- Release the past. This may be easier said than done. Get help if you need it. Spend your energy on the present, while thinking forward to the future.
- Create a positive environment around you. Surround yourself with positive, supportive people whenever possible.
- Manage your emotions. Emotional intelligence is explored in Chapter 5 and 6.
- Start each day with a positive thought.
    - Practice gratitude: Find peace and joy in the things and people around you.
    - Focus on your strengths: See areas that need improvement not as weaknesses but opportunities to grow. Train your mind to focus on what you can achieve every day.
    - Create positive affirmations: Affirmations are uplifting statements such as, "Today will be a great day." Or "I'm showing up as my best self today."
    - Help others: Altruistic deeds help you keep your mind on positive behavior. Plus, it feels good to help others.
- Practice positive visualization. Think how you want your career or life to look, then see yourself in that situation. When you take your mind to a positive place, you'll notice the feeling of pleasure neurotransmitters flowing through your mind and body. Imagine yourself in your dream job

or business venture. What does it look like? How do you feel? Who are you surrounded by? As you visualize yourself in your happy place, pleasure neurotransmitters and hormones such as dopamine, serotonin, oxytocin, and endorphins are released in your brain and throughout your body. Your visualization practice can reduce stress, provide calm, improve your mood, and give you that "high" feeling of positivity. Positive visualization creates a memory as if it were real and helps you focus on your desired future state.

- Celebrate your successes. There is a neurological reason for celebrating success. Dopamine, the neuro-pleasure chemical, is released in your brain when you either achieve something or simply anticipate achieving it. Dopamine is a "feel good" hormone, so you'll want more of those "feel good" moments. Acknowledge your small wins along the way. When you break down your lofty goals into smaller more realistic goals, you give yourself an opportunity to feel good about your progress. Focus on what you've accomplished and celebrate every success. Focusing on success is a technique for cultivating a positive mindset. It also reduces stress. To sum it up, celebration releases happiness!
- Self-care. Take good care of your mental, physical, and spiritual self. There is a powerful connection between your body, mind, and spirit. Self-care is vital for your body and brain to run efficiently. There are many forms of self-care. Discover what works best for you. Get enough sleep, enjoy a healthy diet, exercise, practice meditation, socialize, and build healthy relationships. These are all excellent ways to cultivate and maintain well-being.

KEY CONCEPTS

- ✓ Your mindset arises from your world view or philosophy in life.
- ✓ Mindset determines your interpretation and response to personal experiences and your perception of the world. Mindset is a matter of choice, so how you choose it shapes your relationship with yourself, with others, and your world view. So, choose it wisely.
- ✓ A person's mindset is unique to them. It's your personal perspective or lens through which you observe yourself and the world, shaped by beliefs, assumptions, and thoughts.
- ✓ It is one thing to be motivated by inspiration and it's clearly another to sustain your motivation. Sustained motivation is linked to your beliefs, assumptions, and thoughts – your mindset.
- ✓ *Self-motivation* requires the autonomy to be a causal agent in your life. Knowing you can retrain your brain and change your mindset is powerful.
- ✓ How you view your experience shapes your world. It's a *habit* you develop. Most significantly, it is malleable. Through discoveries in neuroscience, specifically neuroplasticity, we've learned you can change your mind by changing your thoughts.
- ✓ An interpretive process, your mindset is shaped by your internal monologue, or your self-talk. It affects the outcomes in your life in one of two ways by either limiting or liberating your potential.
- ✓ You can change your mindset at any time. It's not necessarily easy, but once you start mastering your mindset, life will become easier and more enjoyable.

YOUR NOTES:

SELF-MOTIVATION IS LINKED TO EMOTIONAL INTELLIGENCE

CHAPTER 5

The Emotional Brain: Using Emotional Intelligence to Develop and Sustain Self-Motivation

"You got to be kidding me! I spent months working on this project. In one fell swoop, in front of my staff and peers, I learn the organization is going a different direction, but thanks anyway for your efforts?" Sam bellowed to his colleague, Mandi. "I'm so angry and frustrated, I can't even see straight. What should I do? They just threw me and all my hard work under the bus!" he raged on. "Obviously, my boss doesn't like me or appreciate all my effort. I'll show him, I'll quit! Why should I even care about this job or the company?" Clearly Sam felt rejected.

"Calm down, Sam. I get you're upset. But, having an emotional meltdown won't get you anywhere," Mandi said, trying to console her distraught colleague. "Let's think it through before you do anything you might regret later."

Mandi perked up a bit and said, "Y'know Sam, this is actually an opportunity to show your leadership skills and validate the promotion you got last year. I recently went to a seminar on "*The Emotional Brain*," where I learned about emotional intelligence. Learning how to identify and manage your emotions not only helps you to get through tough situations, but also helps develop your self-motivation and move forward. Want me to share what I discovered about emotional intelligence?"

"Sure," Sam answered with a sigh, humbling himself a bit.

Mandi explained, "I learned ways to use my brain's capacity to manage my emotions, so I do my job better. After I returned from the seminar, I started using my new skills. I noticed I'm calmer, I make better decisions, and I have better problem-solving skills. My patience, communications, and relationships have all improved. My boss noticed as well. She commented on my last performance review that she's seen growth in my leadership abilities. Oh, and guess who else noticed a difference? My husband! I've seen a positive difference in my personal relationships with people outside work as well. The best thing is, I feel better about who I am, my personal and professional growth, and my future. I feel more passionate about work and see things with more optimism. Also, I've learned not to take things personally but see situations as growth opportunities. Let's face it, now that I understand how the brain works when it comes to our emotions, I have a grip on it, so I'm motivated! I bet by honing your emotional intelligence skills, you would be able to use the power of your emotions to boost your thought processes, your job performance, and your career opportunities."

Fortunately for Mandi's colleague, Sam, she had learned about another superpower, *emotional intelligence*. Based on what she now knows about how to identify and manage her emotions, she not only has grown in her own abilities to manage challenging situations, but she was also able to coach Sam.

WHAT IS EMOTIONAL INTELLIGENCE?

When you think about intellect or intelligence quotient (IQ), who or what comes to mind? You may think of amazingly smart people like Theoretical Physicist and Cosmologist, Stephen W. Hawkins or Chess Grandmaster, Bobby Fischer. Intelligence is often defined as the ability to perceive or infer information, retain it as knowledge, and apply it to critical thinking and problem-solving. The abbreviation "IQ" was coined by the German psychologist William Stern in his 1912 book on assessing human intelligence. Since this term has been used to describe intellectual intelligence for over a century, we've become familiar with its meaning and use in testing levels of intelligence.

When you think about emotional intelligence, what comes to mind? If you draw a blank, you're not alone. Emotional Intelligence, abbreviated "EI" and Emotional Quotient "EQ," refers to the ability to recognize, label, monitor, measure, and manage your emotions as well as those of others. In 1990, Peter

Salovey and John Mayer published a scholarly paper where they coined the term *Emotional Intelligence*. They defined it as, "The ability to monitor one's own and others' emotions and use the information to guide one's thinking and actions." In 1995, the term became popular by Daniel Goleman in his bestselling book *Emotional Intelligence.* Goleman later expanded his definition as, "The capacity for recognizing our own feelings and those of others, for motivating ourselves, and managing emotion in ourselves and our relationships."

According to Goleman, EI taps into the basic element of human behavior distinct from your intellect. He says, "There is no known connection between IQ and EQ; you simply can't predict EQ based on how smart someone is." IQ is cognitive and fixed. It's something you're born with. However, EI is a flexible skill, so the good news is it can be learned and developed. Much like we're able to assess your IQ, today there are well-researched and tested ways to assess EI, known as Emotional Quotient (EQ).

The Difference Between IQ and EQ

IQ	**EQ**
Measurement of an individual's ▶ intellectual, analytical, logical, and rational abilities. ▶ ability to learn new things. ▶ ability to focus on tasks, retain and recall objective information, manipulate and analyze numbers, and solve problems by applying prior knowledge.	Measurement of your ability to ▶ read and respond to political, relational, and social environments. ▶ intuitively grasp what others are feeling and experiencing in the moment, and what they want or need. ▶ remain unruffled by stress. ▶ self-m anage emotions. ▶ tap into common sense–street smarts.
Peaks at around age 15 to 17 and remains fixed through adulthood; however, wanes as we age.	Is not fixed and increases as we mature; however, it can wane slightly as we age.

Whether you're in the role of a leader, employee, parent, pastor, neighbor, politician, or are a student, entrepreneur, athlete, performer, or artist, you're a person first. A person with some level of emotional intelligence. EI is essential to how you express yourself, develop and maintain relationships, cope with challenges and setbacks, make decisions, and solve problems. It's been proven to be a key driver of effective leadership, job performance, and teamwork. EI is the ability to manage your feelings and emotions, using that information to guide your thinking and actions to achieve success and overall well-being.

How much of an impact does EQ have on your professional success? According to researchers, a lot. Your EQ is foundational for a host of critical skills used at work and in your personal lives because it impacts almost everything you say and do. Goleman states, "EQ is so critical to success it accounts for 58 percent of performance in all types of jobs. It's the single biggest predictor of performance in the workplace and the strongest driver of leadership and personal excellence." Research reveals 90 percent of high performers are also high in EQ. As a result, research has found people who measure high in EQ across all industries, at all levels, in every region of the world are higher performers and earn higher annual salaries.

EQ Matters! When you enter the workforce, you typically bring along basic math, reading, and writing skills, plus your knowledge in a particular discipline. However, too often people lack the skills to manage their emotions, especially when they're challenged, or they find themselves in uncomfortable situations. Success requires more than developing expertise in basic skills and knowledge of your profession, it also requires emotional mastery. Mastering your ability to recognize and manage your emotions is a superpower.

WHY EQ MATTERS

Understanding what triggers your feelings and behavior provides you information so you can perform at your best. When you have the ability to accurately observe and identify the emotions triggered within you, and why they're triggered, you can learn to manage your emotions and apply this wisdom to your life:

- Who are you?
- What are your goals, dreams, or aspirations?
- What are your hot buttons?

- What frustrates you?
- Think of a leader who brings out the best in you—what do they do?
- Think of a leader who brings out the worst in you—what do they do?
- In what type of environment do you perform best?

EI isn't about being emotional or being nice all the time. It isn't about being touchy-feely. It's about being honest with yourself and others as well as having the ability to identify, understand, and manage your emotions. It's about being smart with your emotions.

EI matters because it's a superpower. Understanding how EI works and how you can develop your emotional intelligence is linked to your superpowers. How you retrain your brain to think and behave in a way that responds to events and situations appropriately and with intention is how you switch on the positive triggers in your brain. Let's explore how your emotional brain works.

THE SCIENCE OF EMOTIONS

Frustration, anger, disappointment, feeling rejected, dismissed, and devalued: where do our emotions come from? Throughout history, learned men and women in numerous disciplines have always been fascinated about unraveling:

- Where do our emotions come from?
- How do they work?
- What control, if any, do we have over our emotions?

Emotions provide a critical source of information about our environment. They generate distinct feelings. A feeling is a conscious experience or sensation, for instance:

- Emotions signal you that you're in harm's way; therefore, you feel fear.
- You experience something pleasurable; so, you feel happy.
- You suffer an event in opposition to an important desire or need and feel angry.
- You lost something you deeply value; therefore, you feel sad.
- You behaved poorly; as result, you feel shame.

Although there are many words to describe your feelings in any given circumstance, here are the five core emotions: fear, happiness, anger, sadness, and shame. The scale and complexity of these emotions vary in intensity. Typically, more intense emotions are met with a more intense reaction.

With the advent of modern neuroimaging, scientists can study emotions in ways previous generations never thought possible, peering into the brains of living, breathing humans, in real time, as they perceive and experience emotions. Only within the last decade or so have neuroscientists begun exploring how emotions are processed from a neurobiological perspective.

Scientists used to believe the control center of our emotions was in the limbic system, consisting of the amygdala, hippocampus, and other structures in the mid-brain. However, recent advances have revealed emotions involve our whole brain as well as our bodies. Although your limbic system plays a critical role, scientists have discovered your cerebral cortex as well as your body are involved in how you construct emotions.

The limbic system is a warehouse of stored memories that begin at the first breath of life. These memories include impressions and feelings which provide context and meaning to your experiences. These life experiences help you learn and create preferences which guide your behavior. This is where perceptions, preferences, and habits form. You refer to past experiences to predict future events. How you reacted to past experiences influences how you react to future events. You learn to avoid or welcome future events based on past experiences. You conjure up feelings of stress, fear, excitement, and anxiousness as you anticipate what might happen in the future based on your feelings and the meaning you assign to past experiences. So, the limbic system is key to how emotions are stirred. However, the limbic system doesn't operate alone in the initiation or regulation of emotions.

The cerebral cortex region of the brain, where higher thinking happens, is also associated with emotions as it receives information from the limbic system. It's considered your rational brain because it assists with functions related to reasoning, language, decision making, and problem-solving. In tandem with the limbic system, it works to construct meaning and responses to emotions. These two parts of the brain, interconnected by the brain's circuitry, guide, refine, or reject emotional input. As the cerebral cortex receives information from the limbic system, it produces conscious feelings. You could say, this intersection of emotion and higher thinking create emotional intelligence.

Now we can't leave out the rest of your body and its role in your emotions. The brain stem, located just above your spinal cord, not only connects you to the external world through sensory information, but it also regulates your autonomic functions, including your heartbeat, breathing, and nervous system. The millions or even billions of connections between the limbic system, cerebral cortex, and brainstem allow for the free flow of information throughout the brain and body. This system enables you to accumulate emotional data, interpret data, and then, make decisions which guide your responses. Emotional signals in the brain are felt throughout the body. Plus, the body's sensory organs pick up important signals transmitted to the brain. These messages are communicated to and from the body and brain by neurons, traveling through an electrical and chemical transmission system.

Okay take a deep breath. Stand up. Shake your body. Flex your neck and crack your knuckles. It's time to put what you've learned about emotional intelligence to use.

Let's listen in as Mandi helps Sam understand the emotional responses he experienced when his boss rejected his project as well as how he responded a year earlier when he was promoted to Project Manager. Observe what happens when the two separate events triggered emotions.

Event: Your boss informs you the company is going a different direction; therefore, it won't move forward with the project you've worked on at this time.

- You *assess* the event: You worked for months on this, now the project is shelved. To make matters worse, this decision was communicated in front of all your colleagues and team members.
- You *see the event from a perspective associated with memories* stored in your limbic system. You *assign meaning* to the event. Your reasoning mind is temporarily hijacked by negative thoughts of potential negative outcomes. Your ego is bruised, and you feel embarrassed in front of your peers and team members. You fear any future projects might not be accepted, or you could lose your job. Feelings of anger, fear, rejection, disappointment, and frustration are triggered.
- A series of *physiological affects* occur. Stress hormones shoot through your body as if you were confronted by a big grizzly bear in a forest. You experience slight tremors and feel shaky. Your mouth becomes dry and your heart races. More than

likely, your blood pressure increases along with your body temperature. There's a churning sensation in your lower abdomen, and you may have to make a mad dash to the restroom.

- Your *body and facial expression mirror* what's going on inside. Your face turns red. Your body posture stiffens. Your eyebrows scrunch. Your voice cracks. And your leg is shaking uncontrollably under the table.
- You're poised to *react* and engage aggressively.
- Your *mental state* changes, along with your mindset. You transition from a positive mindset anticipating accolades and validation from your boss and peers to a negative mindset as a result of receiving an unexpected rejection and denial instead.

Event: Conversely, when you were promoted to Project Manager last year, your emotional experience was different:

- You *assess* the situation. The promotion brings additional responsibility, an increase in pay, a team of project engineers with whom you'll work, more prestige and visible projects, and a seat at the strategic planning table. This comes with a risk that projects can change based on resources or company direction.
- You *see the event from a perspective associated with memories* stored in your limbic system. You *assign meaning* to the event. Your reasoning mind signals, "This is a good thing. It's progress." The promotion feeds your ego. You'll have more money, power, and a voice. You feel excited and proud. You look forward to buying a new car.
- A series of *physiological affects* take place. You feel a rush of adrenaline, a release of dopamine, oxytocin, and other happy hormones. You're exhilarated and high, like you're walking on air.
- Your *body and facial expression mirror* what's going on within. You're all smiles. Your body posture is relaxed. Your feet barely touch the ground. Your voice is steady, and you speak with confidence, commanding the room.
- You're eager to *respond* with energy and enthusiasm. Your actions are strategic and demonstrate a high level of professionalism.
- Your *mental state* is positive, optimistic, and open-minded.

Mandi applies what she has learned and coaches Sam,

"Sam, you can tap into your superpower and grow as a performer and a leader. Since your brain is wired to be an emotional creature, it's not surprising you react emotionally when a situation triggers your limbic system. When it's triggered, you react spontaneously. You have no control over this part of the process. However, you do control how you experience an incident by how you view it. You also have control over how you respond to the emotions triggered. Learning to shift your mindset and manage your emotions is a game changer. You'll see a difference in your abilities, your job performance, your relationships, and as a leader."

Let's explore what happens during an emotional hijacking, like what happened to Sam. First, I will explain what emotional hijacking is, and then in Chapter 6, I'll discuss how you can address emotional hijacking by growing your emotional intelligence.

Emotional Hijacking

Don't feel like you're in this alone. Everyone experiences emotional hijacking multiple times a day. That's because we all have emotions being triggered by many things. Some are small irritations or stressors such as sitting in traffic; being late for a meeting or waiting on someone else late to a meeting; finding out, once you return to work, you were short-changed by the takeout restaurant where you just bought lunch; or getting ready to board a plane if you're uncomfortable flying. Compare this to other triggers which feel much more significant such as receiving a serious diagnosis from your doctor, or your boss telling you the project you poured your blood, sweat, and tears into was sidelined. These events can trigger high intensity emotions such as anger, fear, disgust, and frustration. By the way, you can also feel high intensity emotions that are connected to love, excitement, and joy.

Why does this happen? In many cases, when you experience negative high intensity emotions, you feel stress due to a lack of control. When you're stuck in traffic or you feel your fate is in someone else's hands like the pilot of the plane or your boss, you experience negative stress. You become quick-tempered, enraged, fearful, or even despondent. When you're put in a stressful situation, your brain function is essentially altered. Your day is humming along just fine, then something happens which triggers a reaction that turns you from a reasonable, jolly person to a primal, irritable person.

The amygdala in the brain, which is located in the limbic system, is key among the emotional centers of the brain. It's the part of the brain that regulates the flight, fight, or freeze response. When your brain is triggered by an event or situation it perceives as dangerous, such as someone confronting you in a dark parking lot demanding your purse or wallet, it shifts into a flight, fight, or freeze stress response. When you're in a flight, fight or freeze state, your brain senses imminent danger. Adrenaline is blasted into your body preparing you to respond to the danger. Emotional hijacking works the same way. When an event triggers you, your reaction activates stress-related responses. Neuroscientists have found when we're triggered, our ability to process information freezes. Hence, the more distress you feel the more likely you are to make snap judgements. These are the moments when you experience strong emotional reactions. During an emotional hijacking, the higher cortex of the brain is disabled, preventing you from making sound, rational decisions. At that point, your emotions take over and you can become reactive, defensive, and lash out at others saying or doing something you may regret later.

Keep in mind, we're all unique and differently wired. Some people are set off by small events like when their mate chews with their mouth open, or they overheard gossip about them during the water cooler talk at work. Other people get worked up over specific topics like religion or politics. That's why it is usually best to stay clear of those topics, especially at work. Other people have a higher level of tolerance for events that can trigger a potential emotional hijacking. The important consideration is to be aware of what hijacks you and learning how to be sensitive to what can trigger others. Preventing emotional hijacking from occurring in the first place is paramount to success in the workplace and in life.

The level at which you control your own stress and emotional hijacking correlates with your level of EQ. The higher your EQ, the quicker you'll identify your own triggers and learn to manage your emotions. The good news is emotional intelligence is like a muscle, it can be strengthened. However, understand strengthening your emotional quotient takes practice. Just as golfer Tiger Woods and swimmer Michael Phelps didn't become world-class athletes overnight, it took the right mindset and lots and lots of practice.

Chapter 6 will address how you can grow your emotional intelligence by shifting your mindset, managing your inner chatter, and developing new thought patterns. But before you address how to manage your emotions, you'll want to develop an awareness of what triggers you. Recognizing stimuli and situations that have the potential to set off your emotions will help you subdue or diffuse a high intensity reaction. Think of occurrences when you feel your blood pressure rising, your heart racing, your brain freezing (a loss of cognitive reasoning i.e., *I was so upset, I couldn't see straight*), or you feel that familiar churning in your stomach. Make a list of those events and how you feel during or immediately after the event such as angry, scared, frustrated, despondent, checked-out, or other emotions.

ACTIVITY # 5

THE EMOTIONAL BRAIN: BEING AWARE OF AN EMOTIONAL HIJACKING.

Reflect on the past and note what triggers you. You can also note immediately after you experience a situation when you were emotionally hijacked.

List things that you know trigger you	What emotions do you feel when you are being triggered?

KEY CONCEPTS

- ✓ The ability to manage your feelings and emotions to guide your thinking and actions to achieve success and overall well-being is at the core of Emotional Intelligence.
- ✓ EI is essential to how you express yourself, develop and maintain relationships, handle challenges and setbacks, make decisions, and solve problems. It's been proven to be a key driver of effective leadership, job performance, and teamwork.
- ✓ The five core emotions include fear, happiness, anger, sadness, and shame. Their complexity and scale vary in intensity. The more intense your emotions, the more likely you'll react with intensity.
- ✓ Recent advances show our emotions involve the whole brain and body. The limbic system plays a critical role, but your cerebral cortex and body are very involved with emotions. Emotions are made by you. You construct your own experiences and your perceptions of others. You're the architect of your experiences.
- ✓ During an emotional hijacking, the higher cortex of the brain is disabled, preventing you from making sound decisions. Your emotions take over and you can become reactive and lash out.
- ✓ You're not in this alone, everyone experiences emotional hijacking multiple times a day.
- ✓ Mastering your ability to recognize and manage your emotions is a superpower!

YOUR NOTES:

HEALTHY EMOTIONAL HABITS LEAD TO SUCCESS IN BOTH PERSONAL AND PROFESSIONAL LIFE

CHAPTER 6

Growing Your EQ:

Taking Steps to Build Your Emotional Intelligence Leads to Improved Performance and Better Relationships

Whether you're connecting with others in the workplace or your personal life, building relationships is at the core of your success. Emotional intelligence is central to forming those healthy relationships. Additionally, developing your emotional intelligence increases your ability to manage chronic stress, improve your resilience, and subdue emotional hijackings or setbacks during challenging events. Finally, EI is linked to increased motivation so you effectively achieve personal and professional success as well as overall good physical and psychological well-being.

EI is an essential competency in many vocations. The value and benefits of emotional intelligence is in forming and developing meaningful relationships as well as managing your psychological health. The Center for Creative Leadership states, "75 percent of careers are derailed for reasons related to emotional competencies, including inability to handle interpersonal problems; unsatisfactory team leadership during times of difficulty or conflict; or inability to adapt to change or elicit trust." Organizations are recognizing the value of employees who exhibit the skills essential to adapt to change, accept constructive feedback with a growth mindset, and work effectively with a team. The bottom line is EI is an important factor in job performance on an individual level as well as within your team.

The good news is it's never too late to grow your emotional quotient. These skills are enabled through self-awareness, which includes understanding from a scientific level what emotions are, where they come from, and how much control you have over them. Then it's a matter of building new constructive thought patterns and turning those thoughts into habits. Let's dive into it!

The knowledge you've gained so far in this book comes into play when you decide to grow your EQ. My friend, this is where the rubber meets the road. Let's do a quick review of what you now know about the brain, positive psychology, and emotional intelligence. Then we'll put everything together and reveal how to successfully tap into your superpowers to master self-motivation.

REVIEW OF KEY CONCEPTS THUS FAR:

- Your *limbic system holds memories of feelings, impressions, and experiences* and banks them for future reference. So, your reaction to your *triggers* is shaped by your history, which also includes your experiences with similar situations.
- The schemas that help you interpret information organize your experiences through *assimilation*. This assigns a thought or experience into an existing category or through *accommodation*, which revises or creates a new category in which to file information.
- *Perception* is your personal sensory experience of the world. It involves recognizing environmental stimuli and prompts behaviors. It includes your physical senses including touch, sight, sound, smell, and taste, as well as your sixth sense, intuition. How you view an incident or episode determines how you experience it. Recall the example from Chapter 4 of two people leaving the mall one evening having different experiences of walking to their car based on how they *framed* their circumstances.
- Your *mindset* works in an interpretive way and is shaped by your internal monologue, your self-talk. Your *internal monologue* explored in Chapter 4 evaluates and judges every observation and piece of information. It's perceived as evidence which either supports or invalidates your beliefs about yourself, others, or the world. It affects the outcomes in your life in two possible ways, by either limiting or liberating you.
- A *growth mindset* is the concept that your intelligence and abilities grow with time, experience, and effort. It doesn't evaluate or judge. It's curious, open-minded,

and has an appetite for exploration and discovery. People with a growth mindset welcome learning and seek information to form new strategies. They're open to inspiration, embracing challenges as opportunities to develop and grow new skills.

- People who experience and express *positive attitudes*, emotions, and behaviors are more likely to be satisfied in life. They're productive and content at work, and they enjoy more rewarding relationships. So, they're more likely to reach desired goals. Additionally, people with a positive attitude, emotions, and behaviors are also more likely to be physically healthier, more resistant to illness, and may even live longer.
- *Negative emotions* hijack your motivation, contributing to increased anxiety and stress. Negative people are less creative, productive, and have greater difficulty with relationships. When negativity spins out of control, they may find themselves in a downward spiral of dysfunction and even depression.
- People with a *victim mindset* ruminate in self-pity. They live in the quicksand and are likely to be reactive versus proactive. They believe they aren't responsible for what they say and do. Instead, they blame others. They spend time and energy complaining rather than doing something constructive. They're likely to procrastinate, avoiding their situation because they're less willing to take risks. They'd rather engage in negative or reactive behaviors then accept their circumstances and move forward.
- People with an *accountability mindset* believe they can manage their career and life. They're proactive about controlling their thoughts and actions. They don't waste time or energy dwelling on "woe is me" thinking. Instead, they focus on what they *can* do and move forward.
- *Neuroplasticity* is your brain's ability to reorganize itself and form new neural connections. It's your nervous system's ability to change its activity in response to stimuli by reorganizing. Your brain is designed to learn, develop, and heal.
- Neuroplasticity is where memory materializes, learning occurs, and experiences are chronicled. When you make connections between ideas and images, your neurons fire encoding ideas and images to memory. Cells that fire together wire together. Neurons firing together *create a neural pathway*. As they fire together, the pathway becomes stronger. The more prolonged the excitation between cells, the stronger the connection and the more likely they are to fire together in the future.
- As firing between your neurons continues, the genes within are turned on to *construct more building blocks* for the neural pathway. This is how you *activate or turn on the switch* in your brain, and it's how *habits* are established. The more

you say, do, and think certain words, behaviors, and thoughts, the pathway is strengthened, and it becomes easier to stick to new habits.

To master your self-motivation, you grow your EQ. As your EI skills grow, you'll discover how to recognize your triggers, manage your response, and practice new ways of responding until they become a natural default. New ways of managing your emotions and behavior become habit. Developing the ability to recognize your emotions and learning to manage them is one of the most impactful skills you can possess. This is one of your superpowers! You'll be able to calm yourself and adjust your behavior to perform better in your career, enjoy healthy relationships, and manage challenges and setbacks with greater ease.

SELF-MANAGEMENT STRATEGIES:

Let's take a deeper dive into Sam's experience from Chapter 5:

- Sam *assessed* the situation and *assumed* the worst. When his boss says, the company's going a different direction from Sam and his team's project, he *assigned meaning* to his boss's words. He took it personally and immediately experienced *emotional hijacking*.
- His *limbic system was triggered* and instantly *sent information to his cerebral cortex*, "Incoming! We're being attacked!"
- His *internal monologue* judges every observation and piece of information as evidence, which supports or doesn't support his beliefs. His *negative self-talk* runs amuck. He says, "Clearly, I'm not good enough! My boss doesn't like me! My projects will never be accepted! I might lose my job! My team sees me as a failure!"
- His verbal outburst and *physiological affects* described earlier only compound the situation.

Sam's *negative emotions* hijack his motivation. They set up a *negative mindset*, which contributes to increased anxiety, stress, and poor performance.

How can he use what's known about the mind and brain to manage and grow his emotional intelligence and transform his lack of motivation to become a self-motivated person?

Here's a snippet of what Mandi discovered in my seminar, *The Emotional Brain,* which she shared with Sam to help him shift from a victim to a leader and regain his motivation.

How to Retrain Your Brain

Retrain your brain by building new neural pathways and developing positive new habits in how you interpret, process, and respond:

BE SELF-AWARE: *By becoming an observer of yourself, your feelings, and how you react or respond, you'll become more mindful of your emotions, impulses, and behaviors. This requires an awareness of your beliefs, assumptions, and thoughts. Yes, it's a challenge to have this presence of mind. But you'll find it's infinitely worthwhile since many emotions, impulses, and behaviors are automatic reactions based on how your brain is wired. This is largely due to the neuropathways strengthened from years of sustained habits. Changing your brain requires making a conscious, cogent effort to break old habits and create new ones. Reflect on the following questions:*

- What's triggering me right now?
- What emotion is being activated?
- What emotional baggage am I experiencing that's influencing my emotional state?
- What assumptions am I making?
  - How might I see this situation from a different perspective?
  - What's positive about this situation?
  - What can I do to be proactive in addressing the situation?
  - What if I change my mindset? What are the possibilities?

PAUSE AND THINK: *It sounds simple, but it's amazing how well this works, especially in difficult or high-anxiety situations:*

- *"Pausing" will make the issue that's just popped up feel much smaller.*
- *"Thinking" will help shift your perspective so you consider how your thought pattern may adversely influence how you affect others (EI).*

Workplace stress on some level is inevitable. A great way to prevent it from impacting you and others is to implement the ten-second rule in interactions and communication. Here's how it works: When you feel triggered, slowly count backward from ten down to one before speaking, responding, or acting. Take ten seconds, a deep breath, and a pause. Is it possible to think of it in a different way? Consider the lens in which you see yourself, the situation, and others involved. You may even need some physical distance away from the situation. Leave the office and take a walk or find a place where you can close the door and decompress. Training yourself to pause before you respond provides essential "breathing time" so you can reset and refresh your thoughts. Then reflect on the following questions:

- Is this perspective serving me to accomplish my goals?
- Am I in a negative or positive mindset?
- How can I look at this situation differently?

Acknowledge any unhelpful thoughts and push them aside. The more you're rooted in negativity, the stronger those neuropathways will become. In contrast, the more you embrace a positive mindset, the stronger those neuropathways become. Eventually, positivity will become a natural, comfortable space where you live. Consider the person you want to be and dwell on the mindset that will help that version of you arrive.

RESPOND VERSUS REACT: *Conscious thoughts often lead to intentional behavior. Under stress, you may misfire, saying things you later regret. When you recognize stress building, you can become intentional about how to manage yourself through the situation. Look at it this way: whether you're exercising, playing with your kids, engaging in a hobby, eating healthy, or practicing your spiritual convictions, you do these things with conscious intention because they make you feel good, positive, healthy, relaxed, and joyful. Approach your challenges with the same intentional conscious thoughts. In many cases, you've trained your brain to live a particular lifestyle. At one point, you may* *have retrained your brain to improve your lifestyle. Maybe you didn't always exercise, eat healthy, or have kids. You changed how you think, behave, and live your life. Neuroplasticity is proof you can train or retrain your brain based on conscious thought and intentional behavior. These examples demonstrate how your mindset structures your lifestyle. They aren't about a single event; they're about how you live your life. Managing your emotional intelligence is a mindset that results in a far better lifestyle. Reflect on the following questions:*

- What do I have control over in this situation? *(Sometimes, the only control you have is how you choose to respond.)*
- Am I on the defensive?
- How can I shift from reacting to responding?
- Can I or should I delay my response? *(Take time to regroup and process.)*
- How can I shift this situation into a positive opportunity using a growth mindset to demonstrate my emotional intelligence, leadership skills, and professionalism?
- Using a growth mindset, ask yourself:
    - What can I learn from this experience?
    - What have I learned from working on the project that equips me for future projects?
    - How can I lead my team with confidence and competence? *(For example, I can provide direction on a path forward that has purpose by establishing new goals aligned with the company's vision.)*

Pulling it All Together

I've covered a great deal about emotional intelligence. Kudos to you for sticking with it. Let me pull together the key take-aways:

Your emotions are created by you. You construct your own emotional experiences, and your perception of others' emotions. You're not at the mercy of mythical emotion circuits buried deep within animalistic parts of your brain. You're the architect of your experience. The good news is you have the power to change your emotions and your results.

The brain receives sensory input from outside and inside your body. Initially, this input is uncategorized and has no psychological meaning. You interpret, assimilate, or accommodate your experiences based on your perception of reality. Many perceptions and your world view are passed down by your parents and influenced by your environment and culture. They influence how you internalize your experiences, creating impressions and feelings. Your brain constructs an internal mental model based on your perceptions and experiences. It's used to make predictions which make sense of sensory input to direct your reaction, action, and predict future experiences, and the cycle continues.

Growing your emotional intelligence requires retraining your brain. You do this by

- observing and being aware of your existing perceptions,
- determining the mindset that best serves you to accomplish your goals,
- shifting your internal dialogue, and
- finally, building new neural pathways.

As you practice and repeat your new skills, you develop new habits. Occasionally old thoughts will come to mind. Recognize them and challenge them if they no longer serve you. Developing new habits is a conscious decision you make followed by your daily actions. At some point it will become your natural default pattern. Habits become a part of your subconscious thoughts, emotions, and behaviors. They'll serve you in sustaining your motivation. This is a superpower!

ACTIVITY #6

GROWING YOUR EMOTIONAL INTELLIGENCE

Next time you're confronted with a situation where you feel you're experiencing an emotional hijacking; use the skills we've discussed for yourself. Observe, pause, and think. Shift your perspective and mindset. Choose to respond in a way that best serves you and others. Reflect on the experience and feel good about how you've taken control of your response.

✓ Growing your emotional intelligence means retraining your brain. Be aware of your existing perceptions, shift your internal dialogue, and build new neural pathways consciously switching off negative or previous thought patterns. Thus, you'll create new ways of thinking and behaving.

▶ Journal your experience below: ______________________________

____

____

____

____

____

____

____

____

____

KEY CONCEPTS:

- ✓ Whether connecting with others at work or in your personal life, building relationships is the core of your success. Emotional intelligence is at the core of building healthy relationships.
- ✓ Developing your EI increases your ability to manage stress, improve resilience, and subdue emotional hijackings when you're triggered.
- ✓ EI is linked to increased motivation to achieve greater success as well as an overall sense of well-being.
- ✓ The ability to recognize your emotions and manage them is a highly impactful skill.
- ✓ You construct your own emotional experiences and perception of others' emotions. So, you can change your emotions and your results.
- ✓ Creating new habits comes from your daily decisions and actions. They'll serve you in sustaining your own motivation. This is a superpower!

YOUR NOTES:

WELLNESS IS A STATE OF GOOD PHYSICAL AND PSYCHOLOGICAL BEING

CHAPTER 7

Well-Being Affects Motivation

Which came first, the chicken or the egg? The chicken, no, the egg, no, the chicken, no, the egg! It's a riddle that's kept us perplexed throughout the ages. Some would argue an egg must come before the chicken, otherwise, how is a chicken born into existence. While others insist you can't have an egg if you don't first have a chicken. If you solved that riddle, you may also be able to solve the riddle, what comes first, motivation or good health? Some contend, you must be motivated to develop and sustain a healthy lifestyle, while others assert motivation comes because of feeling healthy. The answer is both statements are true. We can say with certainty, motivation and good health are circular. Although the chicken argument continues to intrigue us, we can solve the motivation versus good health challenge by working on our mind and body simultaneously.

Good health and motivation both matter because everything you do and every emotion you feel is directly linked to your physical and psychological wellness. There's a crucial connection between your body and your brain that helps you perform at your best. Your brain controls every aspect of your body, health, daily functions, and relationships. Your body affects how well your mind works. If you suffer from foggy thinking, stress, depression, anxiety, exhaustion, forgetfulness, feeling overwhelmed, and other brain-related problems, your mind won't be working at its full potential. Much of brain-related problems come from what we're doing or not doing to our bodies. In this chapter, I'll share with you what I've discovered about the brain-body connection, and how you can use this information to master your self-motivation.

When you're born, your mind is a blank canvas. How you paint the picture of your life is influenced by your thought patterns. Your thoughts and behaviors are habitual, resulting in a lifestyle. Let's face it, as you grow into adulthood, you develop good habits and not-so-good habits that establish your sense of self, which generates your lifestyle.

The hardest part about establishing and sustaining a healthy lifestyle is retraining your brain to think differently. Breaking old habits and creating new ones requires you to switch off old neuropathways and switch on new ones. In the previous chapters, we've explored how the process works and the fact that you have control over your mindset by making choices about how you think and behave. Much like a locomotive control operator switches a railway track to shift the train onto a different track to ensure it's heading in the right direction, when you objectively observe your thinking with the intention of catching unsuitable thoughts, you have an opportunity to switch the track your brain is on to a more suitable *train of thought.*

We've also learned your thoughts have an emotional component. When you think, you also feel. Thoughts occur in your conscious mind, and every thought is linked to your emotions. Emotions are stored in the unconscious mind, triggered by your thoughts. We know emotions have a profound impact on your brain and body. Since science has revealed everything begins with a thought, we can say with certainty, you have the power to choose your future by actively developing new thought patterns that trigger positive emotions. You have an extraordinary ability to determine, achieve, and maintain optimal levels of success when you're healthy and motivated. Having a healthy mind, body, and spirit is key to mastering your motivation.

FOUNDATION OF A HEALTHY BRAIN, BODY, AND MIND

We all know the foundation to good health is rooted in living and enjoying a healthy lifestyle. The fundamentals of living a healthy lifestyle include eating plenty of fruits and veggies, ample sleep, healthy relationships, a spiritual connection, exercise, and having a sense of purpose and meaning in life. Yet, I know from working with my clients, what seems to be common knowledge is not always commonly practiced. It's my belief that if you know a little more about the science behind the relationship linking your brain and body, making changes in your lifestyle will become easier to commit to every day.

General Health for Your Brain, Mind, and Body

I encourage you to work with your doctor to make sure you're aware of and managing any medical conditions that may need a medical doctor's guidance.

Brain, Mind, and Body General Self-Assessment

Reflect on the following questions about the health and wellness you experience and your behaviors relating to your brain, mind, and body.

▶ Brain:

1. Do you experience brain fog (loss of mental sharpness, ability to concentrate, mental fatigue, afternoon blahs, forgetfulness, or not feeling fully present)?
2. Do you have low energy or feel fatigued?
3. Do you rely on coffee or energy drinks to give you some get-up-and-go?
4. Do you have difficulty prioritizing or managing tasks, multi-tasking, or completing your to do list?
5. Do you avoid or procrastinate getting things done?
6. Do you have addictive tendencies with food, alcohol, exercise, social media, or being on your smartphone?

▶ Mind:

1. Do you know what to eat but don't have the discipline to eat the right foods?
2. Do you eat when you're stressed or feel other emotions like anger, anxiety, sadness, or boredom?
3. Do you feel guilty about what or how much you ate?
4. Do you fear becoming fat; therefore, exercise excessively or purge to compensate for overeating food?
5. Do you feel you spend too much time and energy controlling your diet and exercise plan?
6. Do you lash out at others?
7. Do you feel stressed out, have poor relationships, worry about money, feel

isolated, or lonely?

▶ Body:

1. Do you have trouble going to sleep or staying asleep?
2. Is your body mass index greater than 25, or are you unhappy about your weight?
3. Do you have a sluggish immune system (you get sick easily and don't recover quickly)?
4. Do you feel your sex drive is lower than normal for you?
5. Do you struggle with digestive issues (discomfort, gas, constipation, diarrhea or loose stools, heartburn, or leaky gut-bloating/acid reflex)?
6. Do you feel just plain tired all the time?
7. Are you sizing up in your clothes every year?

Tips for a Healthy Lifestyle

1. The key to keeping your brain, mind, and body working is to shut it off for seven to nine hours each night. Sleep is the most important thing you can do to rest and reset your brain.
    a. Your nightly rest is a time for healing and restoration.
    b. Rest builds your resilience and clears out brain fog.
    c. The right amount of sleep can vary for each person, but most Americans do not get enough sleep. When you cut your sleep short, inflammation rises and affects your brain and your body's opportunity to repair and rebuild. This translates into illness, digestive problems, mood swings, and less attention, stamina, strength, and mental clarity.
    d. When you don't get enough sleep, your brain makes more cortisol, which results in feeling anxious and on edge.
2. The food you consume has the potential to help or hurt your gut first, then the brain and body, and, finally, your mind. The food on your fork determines gene expression, hormone levels, immune activity, and even stress levels in your gut, brain, body, and mind. Eat clean to reduce inflammation and clear your

brain of brain fog.

Consider these foods to help you improve your eating habits:

a. Your brain is a major consumer of Vitamin C. Among many benefits to the brain and body, Vitamin C plays a role in the differentiation and maturation of neurons and in the formation of the myelin sheath that protects them. It supports the speed of impulse transmission, making it crucial to cognitive performance.
b. Good fats such as coconut oil, olive oil, avocados, oily fish, olives, and nuts help stabilize blood sugar, so your brain has a steady supply of glucose that's not too high or too low. Healthy omega-3s and omega-6s play a vital role in reducing neuroinflammation and anxiety.
c. Probiotic foods like sauerkraut, miso, kefir, and kimchi help the digestive system. Healthy gut bacteria have been shown to lower LDL cholesterol.
d. Prebiotic foods like bananas, potatoes, oats, apples, and other fiber rich foods support your gut health. Prebiotic slow digestion and help control your appetite as well as provide antioxidants and anti-inflammatory protection.
e. Beef or chicken bone broth help to seal leaky gut issues.
f. Foods such as almonds, cashews, spinach, kale, pumpkin seeds, and avocado are rich in magnesium. Higher levels of endogenous magnesium are associated with lower levels of inflammation.
g. Clean protein, like salmon and other oily fish, and poultry build up calming neurotransmitters.
h. Eat sea vegetables like hijiki, which may block damage to the brain from air pollution.
i. Be sure to include a rainbow of veggies including plenty of dark leafy and vivid colored vegetables in your diet.
j. Stay hydrated. Drinking water helps maintain the balance of body fluids. The function of these fluids includes digestion, absorption, and transportation of nutrients throughout the body, creation of saliva, and regulation of body temperature and circulation. Your brain is strongly influenced by your hydration status. Studies have shown even mild dehydration can impair many aspects of brain function as well as a decrease in energy and motivation.

3. Avoid foods such as:
   a. Caffeine. Caffeine can raise cortisol, which amplifies the fight-flight-freeze response, and rob you of restful sleep. Consider swapping coffee

for green, black, or herbal tea.

b. Sugar and refined carbohydrates can set you up for a roller coaster of anxiety-triggering blood sugar spikes as well as other negative health issues.
c. Processed foods, fast foods, sweets, grains, and alcohol. These foods contribute to a variety of health problems and also are considered depressants. These foods trigger cravings that could lead to addictive patterns.

4. Removing toxins from your diet and environment is critical to your general health. Toxins negatively affect brain development, cell signaling, hormone disruption, cognition, and mitochondrial function. The brain is 60 percent fat, and fat is where toxins hide. Toxins get easily stuck in the brain and stay there unless you actively do something to release them from their little hiding places. You can be exposed to toxins through the foods and drinks you consume and the air you breathe and absorb through your skin. Some of the more common toxins to be aware of include:
   a. Refined vegetable and seed oils; hydrogenated, processed fats in these oils are known to be extremely irritating to the body. Poly-Unsaturated Fatty Acid vegetable oils are prone to oxidation. The oxidation process causes cell mutation, which we see in chronic inflammation, the source of cancer, heart disease, and other illnesses.
   b. Bisphenol-A (BPA); a chemical found in plastic containers of many packaged foods and beverages. Research links BPA to increased blood pressure, and possible adverse effects in the brain and other organs.
   c. Eating high fat (Trans Fat) or the wrong kinds of fats can make the brain leaky, which is associated with negative effects on the digestive tract and even depression.
   d. Heterocyclic Amines (HCAs) and Polycyclic Aromatic Hydrocarbons (PAH) are chemicals formed when muscle meats such as beef, pork, fish, or poultry is cooked using high temperature methods, including pan frying or grilling directly over an open flame. In laboratory experiments these chemicals cause changes in DNA, potentially increasing the risk of cancer.
   e. Refined sugar is linked to breast and colon cancer, obesity, Type 2 diabetes, metabolic syndrome, and fatty liver disease.
   f. Mercury, which is found in certain fish and some plants that grow in mercury-contaminated waters, can be harmful to the body. It can damage the brain's gray matter. Your brain is made up of gray matter and white

matter. Gray matter consists of nerve cell bodies and is where most of the action takes place. It makes up the cortex, where most of your processing and cognition occurs.

5. Consider eating more organic and GMO-free foods, using organic skin-care products, and *green* cleaning and lawn care products. Consider avoiding canned food and plastic water bottles and food containers.
6. When it comes to removing toxins and protecting against future toxin related health risks consider adding vividly colored vegetables, healthy fats, extra dark chocolate, teas, and other foods rich in antioxidants such as berries and Allium vegetables (onions, garlic, and leeks) to your diet.
7. Intermittent fasting can reduce inflammation and lower insulin as well as induce important cellular repair such as removing waste material from cells. When you don't eat for a while, your body makes changes to your hormone levels making stored body fat more accessible. There are also beneficial changes to several genes and molecules related to longevity and protection against disease.
8. Exercise wisely. Exercise improves your health and well-being in many ways. It's a natural mood lifter, it keeps you physically fit and capable, helps prevent illness, improves mental clarity, enhances your emotional well-being, helps reduce stress, increases energy, aides in illness recovery, contributes to living longer, and the list goes on. Exercising a minimum of thirty minutes four times a week is the recommended standard from the medical community. Your exercise plan should include moderate to vigorous exercise, which means bursts of aerobic or high-intensity interval training and resistance or weight training. Consider alternating a brisk walk or jog with a moderate walk, dancing, hiking, kayaking, or other cardio activities.
    a. Regular exercise also lowers leptin. Leptin is a hormone released from fat cells located in adipose tissues. It sends signals to the hypothalamus gland in the brain. Leptin is sometimes called the satiety hormone. It helps inhibit hunger and regulates energy balance, so your body doesn't trigger hunger responses when it doesn't need energy. This hormone helps the body maintain its weight.
    b. Regular exercise also helps lower adiponectin. Adiponectin is a fat-derived hormone that appears to have a critical role in protecting against insulin resistance/diabetes and atherosclerosis (disease of the arteries). Decreased adiponectin levels are thought to play a central role in the development of Type 2 diabetes, obesity, and cardiovascular disease.
    c. To repair leptin and insulin, stop snacking. Eat three healthy meals per day and limit snacking. Enjoy a glass of water or tea in between meals.

Ask yourself, "Am I really hungry? Or, am I bored, tired, angry, or being emotionally hijacked?"

9. Spiritual connection. Practice meditation, prayer, or visualization for five to thirty minutes each day. In addition to being lifted from your spiritual practice, this calming activity normalizes cortisol and reduces inflammation.
10. Connecting to a community and building relationships with like-minded people increases happiness and life satisfaction. Being part of a community improves your psychological well-being. Humans are social creatures. Researchers believe people spend 80 percent of their time in the presence of others, making it important to connect and be in positive relationships. According to the Mental Health Foundation, our need to feel we belong is a major driving force behind our desire to seek out connection. This makes you feel happier, improves feelings of security, and provides meaning to your life. Having relationships affects both mental and physical health.
11. Stress can affect your body, thoughts, feelings, and behavior. Left unchecked, stress can contribute to many health problems, like high blood pressure, heart disease, obesity, a build-up of cortisol (which contributes to belly fat), diabetes, insomnia, headaches, and a variety of illnesses. Effects on your mood can include anxiety, irritability, feeling overwhelmed, sadness or depression, and lack of motivation. Stress effects on your behavior can include overeating or undereating, drug, alcohol, and tobacco use, emotional outbursts, social withdrawal, and isolation. Find ways to manage stress. Consider:

    a. Practice relaxation techniques such as meditation, yoga, tai chi, massage, deep breathing, prayer, spiritual practices, spending time in nature, reading a book, or listening to music.
    b. Get regular exercise or engage in physical activities. Keep moving!
    c. Do something you enjoy such as interesting hobbies, going to a play or concert, playing with your children, or writing a journal, a blog, or even a book.
    d. Spend time with family and friends.
    e. Be sure to get plenty of sleep and eat a healthy, balance diet.
    f. Avoid tobacco and excessive use of caffeine and alcohol.
    g. Finally, reach out for support and get help if you need it.

Being healthy is a superpower to self-motivation. Your health is at the center of your life. Living a healthy lifestyle can not only help prevent long-term illness and chronic diseases, it also can reduce or in many cases eliminate issues that intrude on your motivation such as brain fog, low energy, mood swings, and an inability to concentrate and accomplish tasks and goals. Feeling good about yourself and taking care of your health are important for your self-esteem, self-image, and self-confidence. There is a symbiotic relationship between your health and your motivation. Good health is made up of physical, mental, emotional, and spiritual well-being. Your lifestyle reflects how you intentionally and consciously live every day.

ACTIVITY # 7

ESTABLISHING HEALTHY HABITS ONE CHANGE AT A TIME

Whether you have significant changes or minor changes you want to make to improve your health and well-being, start with small steps.

Remember, small habits lead to big changes. Making behavioral changes can be as simple as turning off your phone and all other devices 30 minutes before bedtime. Here are a few other small changes that can really add up:

- *Plan your meals for the next day.*
- *Sit down when you eat versus eating on the run or on the drive.*
- *Turn a sit-down meeting into a walking meeting.*
- *Take a few minutes when you wake up in the morning to declare a positive outlook.*
- *Say a prayer or meditate.*
- *Write in your journal at bedtime three things for which you're grateful.*
- *Carve out time to engage in a hobby.*
- *Spend time in play with family or friends rather than TV or time on your device.*

Be creative, intentional, and committed to improving your lifestyle. Apply what you've discovered in this book about shifting your mindset, creating new neuropathways, paying attention to your triggers, and managing emotional hijacking to set your self-motivation into action.

FIRST: Prioritize the most important change you want or need to make in your lifestyle. You don't have to do them all at once. Start with one change at a time, if you'd like.

1. ______________________________

____

2. ______________________________

____

3. ______________________________

____

SECOND: Establish the habit. What will you do differently to make a change? How will it benefit you? What cues and processes can you put in place to implement the change?

____

____

____

THIRD: Get Support. Who can you enlist? What system can you put in place to support you in making a change?

____

____

____

FOURTH: Acknowledge progress. Reflect on your progress, celebrate your accomplishments, or adjust your behavior, as necessary.

Use the following table, if you'd like.

GETTING HEALTHY

BRAIN, BODY, AND SPIRIT

HABIT	CUES	SUPPORT SYSTEM
First Habit		
Second Habit		
Third Habit		
Fourth Habit		

Good Luck! I know you can do this!

KEY CONCEPTS:

- ✓ Motivation and good health are circular.
- ✓ Good health and motivation both matter because everything you do and every emotion you feel is directly linked to your physical and psychological wellness.
- ✓ Good health is made up of physical, mental, emotional, and spiritual well-being.
- ✓ Your thoughts and behaviors are habitual, resulting in a lifestyle.
- ✓ The hardest part about sustaining a healthy lifestyle is retraining your brain to think differently. Breaking old habits and creating new ones requires you to switch off old neuropathways and switch on new ones.
- ✓ Your lifestyle reflects how you intentionally and consciously live every day.
- ✓ Small habits lead to big changes.
- ✓ Having a healthy mind, body, and spirit is key to mastering your motivation.
- ✓ Being healthy is a superpower to self-motivation.

YOUR NOTES:

“IT IS NOT ENOUGH TO HAVE A GOOD MIND; THE MAIN THING IS TO USE IT.”

-Descartes

CHAPTER 8

Mental Performance: Breaking the Boredom Barrier

It's Monday, you're in a deep slumber, only to be jarred awake by the piercing sound of your alarm clock. You drag yourself out of bed and shuffle to the kitchen for that first cup of morning joe. As your brain starts to calibrate, you contemplate the day ahead. You're overcome with a sense of dread. The same traffic jam awaits you. There's always an accident on the interstate. You ask yourself, why can't people just stay in their lane and drive? You get to the office, fill up your oversized cup with more coffee, you know, the bright yellow one with the smiley face. You meander back to your "spacious and attractively decorated" workstation. Then check emails, phone messages, and scan your social media accounts once more before psyching yourself up to finally start another day of work. This was Mandi's story.

As a motivation coach, I've heard this narrative more times than I can possibly count. If her story sounds familiar, chances are you're feeling bored at work. You're looking for ways to get motivated and get moving. In this chapter, I'll address why you get bored, and what to do when you're bored at work.

Let's face it, boredom happens to everyone at some point to some degree. According to a recent study published by Udemy for Business, 43 percent of workers report feeling bored at work. The research found more women than men report workplace boredom (48 percent vs. 39 percent) and Millennials are almost double as likely to be bored. Trust me, it's normal to have career lulls or get caught in a rut at your job and as a result become restless and bored. However, if you don't address your boredom, it will take its toll on your career, as well as your mental and physical well-being. Boredom often translates into low productivity at work, poor concentration, and developing bad habits such as drinking alcohol or consuming other feel-good drugs to escape reality, poor eating habits, anxiety, depression, and stress. Something as simple as boredom at work can have severe consequences. But you can turn things around. Let's begin by addressing a few reasons why you may feel bored at work.

Why you may feel bored at work:

- You're not challenged with your work.
- Your interests and talents aren't an ideal match with the work you are doing.
- You have too much down time.
- You don't have clear career or performance goals.
- You're burnt-out and simply find it impossible to perform at your past level.
- You feel exhausted or tired all the time.
- You're checked out due to a lack of inspiration or motivation.
- You're experiencing poor mental or physical health.

Boredom is a common human experience. But how you handle feeling bored makes the difference between succumbing to boredom or taking control of your situation. It's helpful to understand the science behind boredom so you can use self-motivation to manage your situation.

BOREDOM

Your brain is designed to respond to an enormous array of information happening simultaneously from both external and internal stimuli. For example, when driving a car, you're paying attention to all the aspects of driving a car. Meanwhile, you feel the warmth and calm of sunshine on your face. You can quickly smash your foot on the brake to avoid a squirrel dashing across the street. You can hear the sound of an approaching fire truck that triggers you to be on high alert, while listening to your spouse tell you about their day. At the same time, your inner dialogue is having its own sidebar conversation. You fight off an incoming sneeze triggered by looking into the sun. You notice pangs of hunger since you skipped lunch, all while your body maintains its autonomic duties of regulating your heartbeat, body temperature, and blood pressure.

The miracle of our human brain is it's capable of processing a vast number of stimuli simultaneously. It may seem your brain is quite busy, yet it needs a certain amount of stimulation and information to maintain its organization. When there is too much or too little stimuli, you can experience stress. Neither an overtaxed brain nor a bored brain is a happy brain.

The maturing brain develops the capacity to better organize the world. As a baby you were stimulated by your mom's smile, the movement of the mobile dangling above your crib, the urge to release breakfast, and then, demand a diaper change. That was a busy day. As your brain developed and matured, you continuously moved the setpoints needed for stimulation. Think back to how challenging it was starting a new job. There was probably a fairly steep learning curve. There were many things for your brain to adjust to, from navigating your new route to work, to where to park, and how to find your workstation. Once at work, you must learn your job responsibilities and develop relationships. After you have been in your job for a while, your brain adapted to and assimilated many of those elements. Eventually they became mundane and routine. Gradually boredom set in and you can feel your motivation heading down a slippery slope. We all need a degree of challenge to keep us interested, stimulated, and engaged.

Studies have linked boredom to anxiety, depression, and some diseases. All of these can be a root cause for fading motivation. You may think, I'm bored, it's time to get a new job. But that may be unnecessary. It's time to activate your brain in other ways. Learning to cope with your inevitable boredom by stimulating your brain is another superpower to master self-motivation.

Keeping your brain fit includes both maintaining general good health, which was discussed in Chapter 7, and challenging your brain to learn and grow. As mentioned before, your brain is like a muscle, if left dormant it will atrophy. To stimulate your brain, welcome new interactions, challenges, experiences, and ideas. A fit brain allows you to develop your talents, gifts, and realize your full potential.

Okay, like with other efforts to develop mastery, the first task to improve your mental performance related to brain boredom is your level of awareness. Ask yourself:

1. How often do you say or think to yourself, "I'm bored?"

   A. Almost never
   B. Often
   C. Once in a while
   D. Most of the time

2. How often do you intentionally challenge yourself? For example, how often do you learn a new skill, travel to a place you've never visited before, initiate a new relationship, play a game, or engage in a physical or mental activity that stretches your comfort zone?

   A. Almost never
   B. Often
   C. Once in a while
   D. Most of the time

3. How often do you purposely do something different outside your daily routine like taking a different route to work, reading a book from a different genre, trying a new restaurant or food choice, or strike up a conversation with a total stranger while waiting in line at the grocery store?

   A. Almost never
   B. Often
   C. Once in a while
   D. Most of the time

4. Do you fully engage yourself mentally in your work?

   A. Almost never
   B. Often
   C. Once in a while
   D. Most of the time

5. Do you look for or ask to participate in special projects, community service programs, or other committees at work?

   A. Almost never
   B. Often
   C. Once in a while
   D. Most of the time

6. Do you avoid tasks or getting started on a project by procrastinating or looking for distractions like scanning your social media apps?

   A. Almost never
   B. Often
   C. Once in a while
   D. Most of the time

7. Do you daydream or visualize future events?

   A. Almost never
   B. Often
   C. Once in a while
   D. Most of the time

8. Do you actively plan and initiate what happens in your life?

   A. Almost never
   B. Often
   C. Once in a while
   D. Most of the time

9. Do you avoid problem-solving, decision-making, or getting involved in complex issues?

   A. Almost never
   B. Often
   C. Once in a while
   D. Most of the time

10. Do you avoid initiating new activities or projects?

   A. Almost never
   B. Often
   C. Once in a while
   D. Most of the time

The purpose of these questions is to get you thinking about how well you are exercising your brain muscle every day. Now, some may say finding creative ways to get out of work early is exercising your brain. Yes, that may be true to a certain extent, however, it defeats the purpose of mastering your self-motivation. I view brain exercise almost like regular physical exercise. Challenging yourself to experience new things or stretching your comfort zone releases the motivation hormone dopamine as you anticipate a sense of accomplishment, much like a runner experiences a release of endorphins, referred to as a "runner's high."

Your personal success happens when you're at your personal best. To experience your personal best, start by developing your mental skills.

MENTAL SKILLS

What do basketball great Michael Jordon, legendary entertainer Celine Dion, world renowned cellist, Yo-Yo Ma, business mogul Sara Blakely of Spanx fame all have in common? They, among countless other highly successful people, realized their dreams by having the mental skills essential to achieve success. Those mental skills include:

- Choosing a positive attitude – Seeing challenges as opportunities.
- Using mental imagery – Visualizing your success.
- Using positive self-talk – Encouraging yourself as you would your best friend.
- Managing your emotions – Developing emotional intelligence to use emotions to inspire rather than interfere with high-level performance.
- Having a growth mindset – Having a willingness to learn and stretch your comfort zone.
- Managing stress and anxiety effectively – Realizing some anxiety is natural and can help you perform at your best.

- Maintaining concentration and focus on the task at hand as well as the bigger goal – Knowing how to maintain focus and resist distraction and procrastination.
- Disciplining yourself to deal with the pain and boredom that comes with repetition – Remaining in the present while keeping an eye on the prize.
- Maintaining a high-level of self-motivation – Persisting through difficult tasks, boredom, and challenges even when the rewards aren't immediately forthcoming.

While everyone has varying talents, you can develop the mental skills to reach your full potential. These mental skills are necessary to sustain daily practice as well as growing and increasing your abilities over long periods of time. It often takes years to attain long-term goals. Successful people have the mindset to stick with their daily routine and repetition of training, practicing, and learning. The greats never show up late and leave early. They don't scan their social media several times or surf the internet every time their mind begins to wander.

Boredom can easily creep into your mindset and impact your performance. This happens because you allow your mind to wander. Also, because you lack dedication and focus on your longer-term purpose or goals. Allowing your mind to wander and let boredom set in will rob you of the opportunity to reach your full potential.

TIPS TO BREAK THE BOREDOM BARRIER

Boredom won't go away unless you act. So, here are some suggestions to help you break through the boredom barrier:

1. Know yourself and your passions. What gets you up in the morning? It's important to stay connected to what provides meaning and purpose in your life. Keep your dreams alive by watering and nurturing the seeds you're planting in your life. Everything you do today prepares you for the future. Shift your mindset to see what seems to be a mundane task as a building block for your future. This will engage you in the task at hand. Remember, even when a seed is planted, it requires nutrients from the soil. It must be watered regularly, and mostly, it requires patience before you can reap the fruit of its work. Keep your eye on the prize!
2. Establish your goals. Having clearly defined goals provides direction, a path, and a plan. Your goals become your *why*. Why you get up in the morning? Why you go to work? How will what you're doing now help you achieve your long-term dreams? Establish small, short-term goals as well as long-term ones. Achieving smaller goals provides success that gives you spurts of the motivation hormone

dopamine. Before you know it, you'll realize your bigger dream. I call it having bifocal vision. Keep your eye on your short-term goals while also keeping your long-term goals in view.

3. Create excitement in your life. Do things you enjoy and enjoy the things you do. For example, make exercise fun to help you achieve your health goals. Find physical activities that'll keep you fit, and you find enjoyable. Do you have a competitive spirit? Do you like competing with others or with yourself? Maybe you prefer a team sport, walking with a buddy, or flying solo. Find what rocks your world. When you do, you'll stick to it and see the results. Build relationships with others who share your interest, as well as having a curiosity and willingness to try new things.
4. Stretch yourself at work. To stay inspired and motivated, find activities that excite you in your organization. Consider finding a mentor or being a mentor. Find ways to improve how your work process gets done. See the nuances in what you do and appreciate how they contribute to the bigger picture. If your job is assembling brakes on cars, imagine a family driving safely to church on a sunny Sunday morning or the dog to the dog park. Assign value and meaning to what you do. Learn new skills. Volunteer for committees. Get involved in work-related community events. Cross-train for another position that could move you up. Attend trainings inside or outside your work. Create career goals and a path to achieve your goals. Find work you love by following your passion, talents, and interests.
5. Spend time with the right people. Your circle of family, friends, and co-workers can influence how you view your life and ultimately how you live your life. Hang out with people who are positive, role-models who challenge you at times and inspire you all the time.
6. Find value and be valuable. See the value you bring to your job, co-workers, family, and friends. Be someone's hero by showing them that you care about them, while you encourage and support them. Inspire others by being a role-model. Challenge others to rise up and accomplish their personal best.
7. Live each day as if you knew this was your last day. Guess what? We all die someday. As morbid as that sounds, many people who are diagnosed with a serious medical condition or those who have a close brush with a catastrophic event often get a big wake-up call and start living their best life at that point.
8. Communicate with your supervisor. It's amazing how often people wait for someone else to notice, address, and take-action on their behalf. Speak up. Take the initiative to have a conversation with your boss and express your desire to learn and grow. Find work that better fits your interests, talents, and goals, or take on new challenges.
9. Know what you want from your job and what your opportunities are with the

company for which you work. If you've exhausted all efforts in your job to break the boredom barrier, it may be time to move on and find a position or company that's a better fit for your current needs and your potential development. You may want to seek career advice to help you navigate your career planning.

10. If you are an entrepreneur and you feel like you're in a rut, try something new. Mix up your day. Create a new marketing approach. Look for ways to improve on your product or services. Seek out other entrepreneurs with whom you can share experiences.
11. Check in with your physical and mental health. Are you eating a well-balanced diet, sleeping, exercising, and playing enough? If you feel burnt-out, take short breaks to refresh throughout the day. Take that much needed, often overdue, vacation. Find what works for you and establish new habits.
12. Collaborate with others. If you work alone, you may find yourself getting bored as a by-product of your loneliness. Even if you're naturally a loner, research tells us people need people. We all need a degree of socialization and collaboration. Look for opportunities to work with other teams or people in your network. Interaction with other people generates the release of oxytocin, a "feel-good" hormone. In addition, interacting with others helps you to acquire new skills, share your expertise, fosters feelings of purpose and value, and fuels your creativity. Spend time getting to know your co-workers and create meaningful relationships at work. Engage in group activities, even if it's over a Zoom call.
13. Take steps to improve your emotional intelligence. Practice self-awareness while maintaining a positive mindset. Don't blame others or your job for your feelings. If you feel bored, overwhelmed, frustrated, or anxious take control of those feelings by addressing and managing your thought patterns and your environment.
14. Gamify your work. Gamification is a new concept, growing in popularity. The idea is to add gaming elements to everyday work life. You can create games with your co-workers, awarding points as it relates to getting work done. The winners receive prizes like a free lunch the next time everyone goes out to lunch. It's a great way to be creative and make work more fun.
15. Be curious. Look at the world from a new lens. See things from the customer's point of view. Try new things and ask questions. See yourself as the director of your own movie:
    - Where is the set?
    - What is the storyline?
    - How will it end?
16. Explore a new hobby. Research a new way of doing your work, a new system, product, devise, etc.

ACTIVITY #8

BREAKING THE BOREDOM BARRIER

Boredom can be due to being too busy or not busy enough. Either scenario can cause you to check out. Also, boredom at work is not always a bad thing if it leads to beneficial action. In fact, research shows being bored at work can be a trigger that moves you to act, become more productive, creative, and engaged. Follow these steps to address and manage boredom at work:

STEP 1: Awareness: *Reflect on the root cause of your boredom.*

STEP 2: Mental Skills: *Examine what mental skills you need to develop.*

STEP 3: Act: *Put into action new thought patterns, mental skills, and efforts to address and manage the root cause of your boredom. Get out of your own way!*

KEY CONCEPTS

- ✓ Boredom is a common human experience. How you handle feeling bored makes the difference between succumbing to boredom or taking control of your situation.
- ✓ The brain is capable of processing a vast number of stimuli simultaneously. Although it seems your brain is quite busy, it needs a certain amount of stimulation and information to maintain organization. When there is either too much or too little, you may experience stress.
- ✓ Studies link boredom to anxiety, depression, and some diseases. All can be a root cause for fading motivation.
- ✓ Your brain is like a muscle; left dormant it will atrophy. To stimulate your brain, welcome new interactions, challenges, experiences, and ideas. A fit brain allows you to develop your talents and gifts and realize your full potential.
- ✓ Challenging yourself to experience new things or stretching your comfort zone releases the motivation hormone dopamine as you anticipate experiencing a sense of accomplishment.
- ✓ Boredom can easily creep into your mindset and impact your performance. Allowing your mind to wander so boredom sets in robs you of the opportunity to reach your full potential.
- ✓ Coping with boredom by stimulating your brain is another superpower to mastering self-motivation.

YOUR NOTES:

STOP LIVING IN THE SUFFOCATING SPACE OF SELF-THREAT AND EMERGE INTO THE SPACE OF SELF-MOTIVATION

CHAPTER 9

Your Head Voice: How to Talk to Yourself and Why it Matters.

ARE YOU GETTING IN YOUR OWN WAY?

I've prepared for this interview.

I'm ready for this interview.

I know I can do the job.

What if they ask me something I don't have an answer for, or what if I don't have the right experience?

What if I'm not the best candidate for the job?

The other person in the waiting area was wearing a very expensive suit.

Maybe I'm underdressed.

What if they don't like me?

What if I don't get the job?

How will I pay my bills?

My hands are sweating, my stomach is in knots, and my heart is racing! My brain is in total panic. Just as they call me back, I feel an urge to use the restroom.

Mandi shared her experience with me when she recalled her interview. She described what it felt like moving from feeling calm, confident, and prepared to feeling overwhelmed and anxious. Her shift in perspective was a result of her own self-induced fear. Mandi's emotionally based fear was activated by a perception she's not good enough, she surely will fail, she won't be accepted, and as a result she won't be able to pay her bills. She explained, in the moment, she felt her life was over. In this example, Mandi digressed from feeling competent and confident to feeling anxiety and physical distress. Her self-talk and thoughts created an emotional stress trigger that caused her brain to activate the survival stress hormones adrenaline and cortisol.

Researchers estimate we think about 50,000 to 70,000 thoughts a day. Up to 80 percent of those thoughts are negative. That's a crazy amount of negative self-talk. Let's be frank, your negative self-talk is downright self-destructive. Your thoughts greatly influence how you feel and behave. Telling yourself you're not good enough over and over will eventually manifest itself into your truth. Your feelings of low self-worth will get in the way of achieving your goals.

We all experience the voice in our head. At times, it can help us keep motivated, pushing toward our goals; like when it reminds us not to reach for that donut because it's not on our diet. Or, we have a debate in our head about overspending too much for a new pair of shoes when we're saving for a car. The question I'll address in this chapter is how to use your self-talk as an effective tool to master self-motivation.

MEET YOUR HEAD VOICE

From the time you're able to hear, interpret, and reflect on the external voices you hear, and physical expressions you observe, you begin developing language by assigning meaning to words and expressions. If you're like most children, the first voices you hear are those of your parents. In the beginning, the conversations are mostly about how cute and precious you are. Then your big brother comes along and in a jealous rage says you're nothing more than a nuisance, and he wishes you were never born. In your impressionable young state, you internalize these messages.

Scientists studying the *inner voice,* the one in your head, say it takes shape in early childhood and persists throughout our lifetime. As children, we learn to self-relate by how we're spoken to and treated by our parents, caregivers, family members, teachers, peers, and other influential people in our lives. When those people treat us with love, acceptance, respect, and care, we learn self-love, self-acceptance, self-respect, and self-care. However, if we miss out on these positive utterances, or worse, are surrounded with negative words that are disrespectful, condescending, dismissive, neglectful, or abusive, we learn to treat ourselves the same way.

Your Inner Voice Begins as Audible Self-Talk in Your Toddler Years.

Children begin audible self-talk as they learn new sounds and practice sounding out words and putting together sentences. They engage in self-talk during play, often taking on the role of more than one imaginary character. They use their newly discovered tool of language and self-talk to direct and regulate play and behavior. For example, a child may use their inner voice to direct their imagination while building a tower of building blocks. "This block goes here, and this one goes over here," they say. Suddenly the project takes an unfortunate turn. "Oh no, it fell down. I have to start over. But I don't want to. It's too hard. I can't do it. I'll play with something else." Or, "Oh well, it fell down. I'll start again, but this time, I'll use bigger blocks at the bottom of the tower to keep it standing better." The practice of putting thoughts into words is how self-talk is born. Children learn these skills through their parents, caregivers, and play partners at an early age. Then, they go off on their own talking themselves through tasks. At some point, children internalize their self-talk until it's mostly silent. It becomes an on-going internal dialogue that continues to live within a person the rest of their life.

Born from experiences internalized during the formative years, self-talk is fueled by those who influence learning and play. In the best scenario, the patient, positive caregiver provides you with encouragement using words like, "You can do it—try again." This builds self-esteem and provides you with a personal source of positive self-talk to draw upon when you run up against life's trials and thorny moments. It provides the tools to guide you through the most challenging problems. By contrast, an abrupt impatient caregiver may contribute to a negative pattern of self-defeating self-talk. If a caregiver blurts out, "You idiot, you can't do anything!" In this case, you're more likely to give up, experiencing a sense of frustration and failure. These early negative experiences promote self-judgement, self-criticism, or doubts about your abilities. This psychological construct is known as the *Inner Critic*. Unfortunately, excessive self-criticism can become a dominant negative influence in your life.

FRIEND OR FOE: BE YOUR OWN BEST FRIEND OR YOUR OWN WORST ENEMY

I'm too old. Too fat. Too stupid. Too lazy. I'm an imposter. I'm not good enough. You should've done this or that. Why didn't you just say this or that? What's wrong with you? Your head voice can be your foe.

We've all experienced that head voice expressing criticism, frustration, or disapproval. Herein lies the inner critic. It attacks and undermines you to protect you from the shame of failure. This self-talk links back to a time when we feared disapproval and rejection from caregivers including siblings, teachers, or other influential people in our life. Shame is the feeling you're not worthy, competent, or good enough. People do this because the inner critic believes it is doing what's necessary to protect you from disappointing yourself or others. If you convince yourself not to try, then in theory, you can't fail. Our biological response to danger is fight, flight, or freeze. The inner critic reads failure as real-life danger. It triggers us to avoid or reduce risks to stay safe and protect ourselves. Unfortunately, this inner dialogue is anxiety provoking and shaming, which is a killer to our self-motivation.

In coaching, the inner critic is called your *monkey-mind*. According to Buddhist principles, the *monkey-mind* is a term referring to feeling unsettled or confused. It's the part of your brain connected to ego, which insists you can't do anything right, you're not good enough. It stifles creativity, performance, and motivation. The monkey-mind is your foe.

Everyone engages in self-talk. But whether it hurts or harms you depends on how you do it. Scientists have discovered changing how you talk to yourself can free you from the space of suffocating in negativity and shame and emerge in a space of self-motivation.

Your head voice can be your best friend; a powerful ally to help you succeed in life. When your head voice is your *believer* and advocates for you, you feel like you can achieve anything. Think back to a time when you first tried something and succeeded, what was going on in your head? Maybe it was when you finally soared down the street on your bike fully balanced, free of training wheels. It was probably one of the most freeing, exhilarating feeling you ever felt as a child. In that moment, your head voice cheered on your success saying, "I knew you could do it! You can do anything you put your mind to!"

I remember studying hard for my driver's test, and my mom spending countless hours coaching me through driving on snow and ice, in parking lots, on neighborhood streets, and highways. I failed the first two times I took the test. I believed if everyone else on the road (some who shouldn't be driving) could get their license, I could do it too, and I did! The third time was the charm. I passed! Your believer is your friend.

Shutting down your inner critic, the monkey-mind, who always second guesses your abilities or reminds you of your flaws, will help you gain confidence, so you'll achieve your goals. How do you shut down the monkey mind and advance your believer?

STEPS TO SHUTTING DOWN YOUR WORST ENEMY AND PROMOTING YOUR BEST FRIEND

Step 1: Develop an Awareness of Your Thoughts

Becoming aware of your thoughts is the first step to recognize, identify, and then let go of your inner critic. Next time you feel anxious, not good enough or fear-ful, acknowledge the voice in your head as your monkey mind. Ask yourself:

- What is it about this situation that upsets me?

- What am I afraid of?
- What would it mean if what I'm afraid of happened?
- What about this situation is leaving me feeling vulnerable?

The answer to these questions is what your inner critic is protecting you from feeling. Ask yourself if you really need that protection? What's the trade off if you withdraw and don't try or grow? Pay attention to your thoughts. Just because you're thinking those thoughts doesn't make them true.

Step 2: Employ Proactive Techniques to Manage Your Head Voice

Self-Distance

Although it's nearly impossible to completely shut down your inner critic, you can keep it at bay. Researcher, Ethan Kross of the University of Michigan's Emotion & Self-Control Lab, and his colleague Ozlem Ayduk of the University of California, Berkeley, suggest the best way to respond to your inner critic is from a detached perspective, as if you were another person. This technique is called self-distancing. To self-distance you replace the first-person pronoun, "I" with a third person reference. You can assign your inner critic its own name such as referring to it as your monkey mind, or you can call it by your own name or make up a fun name.

In Mandi's case, she would say to her inner critic, "Mandi, why are you bothering me with this silliness. You know I'm prepared for this interview, and I've got this, so leave me alone." This shift works especially well when you're beating yourself up, Kross found. He explains how self-distancing works. Instead of feeling unworthy of getting the job as you recount an experience from the first-person perspective, self-distancing allows you to pause, step back, and think as clearly and rationally as if the situation was happening to someone else. This enables self-control and allows you to think clearly, performing with confidence.

Taming Your Monkey-Mind

Another technique is to refer to your inner critic as your monkey mind. Since your monkey mind is attached to your ego, its purpose is to protect you from what it views as harm. It's on your side, looking out for your best interest, misguided though it may be. Your monkey-mind tries to protect you from blows to your ego. Imagine this monkey lives in a little basket in your mind. It jumps out of the basket when it sees an opportunity to fill you with self-doubt. You know, the self-doubt in your subconscious put there during your childhood. When your monkey mind jumps out of the subconscious basket politely say, "Thank you for sharing your thoughts and trying to protect me, now get back in your baskct."

Reframe Your Thoughts

After you send your monkey packing, reframe your thoughts. Using self-affirmation is useful for most people to offset self-criticism. When you hear your monkey-mind spout negative thoughts, redirect your thoughts, reflect on your strengths, abilities, talents, and previous success stories. Affirmations can change up the negative messages held hostage in your head voice from the past. They help you reframe them to the present and what you imagine as your future. Using this technique, you shift the emphasis from the past to the present, acknowledging who you're becoming and how you'll continue to grow. Studies show affirmations are useful at showing you a range of possibilities. They're considered *cognitive expanders*. They help you bolster self-worth and widen your vision of yourself. You then see your full potential more clearly.

The Good-ish Concept

Dolly Chugh, a social psychologist at New York University's Stern School of Business suggests, instead of thinking of yourself in binary terms as "good" or "bad," think of yourself as *good-ish*, a term she introduced in her book, *The Person You Mean to Be.* She explains, good-ish embraces the notion you're prone to errors and have internal conflict; however, you instinctively do your best to be better. By taking on the good-ish concept, you see yourself as a work in progress. Good-ish encourages you to take risks, make mistakes, and, most important, learn from those mistakes. To make this shift, Chugh advises you to activate a growth mindset that triggers a growth-oriented inner voice as opposed to an endless inner critic voice.

Mandi's inner critic head voice said she wasn't ready for the interview or good enough to get the job. However, a growth-oriented voice would respond with positive reassurance saying, "*You're ready for the opportunity. Do your best!*" If she didn't get the job, her growth-oriented inner voice would follow up with kindness, self-compassion, and encouragement by saying, "*What can you learn from this experience to better prepare yourself for the next opportunity*?" The technique begins with a conscious choice to allow your growth-oriented voice speak louder than your inner critic.

Be Your Own Best Friend

Another technique is asking yourself what advice you would give your best friend. Imagine if your best friend said to you, "I have an interview tomorrow, and I'm nervous."

Would you say, "You'll never get the job. You're too stupid. You probably won't answer questions very well because you don't have the right experience." I would hope you wouldn't say such things. If you did, you may not have very many friends for long. You're more likely to offer your best friend words of encouragement like, "You got this! You've prepared for the interview, you have extensive experience, and you have a great work ethic. And guess what, if it doesn't work out, I'll be here as your friend to help you prepare for the next opportunity. Now go get'em! Knock their socks off!" Talk to yourself in a way that's equally as kind and encouraging as you would to your best friend.

Examine the Evidence: Be Rational and Realistic.

It's okay to be rational, realistic, and examine the evidence. Your head voice can take you down a path full of misinformation about your talents. Learn to recognize when this happens and shift into detective mode. Draw a line down the middle of a piece of paper. On the left-side list all the attributes and evidence you have that support your success. On the right-side list any evidence to the contrary. Reviewing the hard evidence from a rational perspective can help you look at your situation realistically and less emotionally. This technique minimizes the tendency for your head voice to exaggerate negative thoughts or be overly optimistic. Unrealistic optimism can be devastating if a situation doesn't work out as you hoped. Keeping it real may be the best approach for your personality type.

Use Your Past Success Stories to Build Your Confidence

"The past has infinite value if one learns from it." –Ken Hensley

Using experience as a resource to build your confidence can change your future. When confronted with a new experience that feels uncomfortable, think about a previous experience when you felt anxious but made it through with grace and style. Think about the first day on the job. It's typically full of angst and uncertainties like:

- What should I wear?
- Where will I park?
- Should I bring lunch, or will someone take me to lunch on my first day?
- Where will my work area be?
- Will anyone talk to me?
- What will I need to learn to do my job well?
- What if I mess up on my first day?

Almost endless opportunities for your monkey mind to jump out of its basket! Once you've been in the job for a while, and you reflect on that first day, you'll probably chuckle thinking about how much you worried. Somehow you made it through that first day and moved on with grace and style. Whatever is in front of you giving you feelings of trepidation now, see it as temporary. It's just a blip in your life's chart. You succeeded in the past and you'll succeed in the future.

Think about a time you made a mistake. What was the worst thing that happened? Somehow you survived it and learned lessons from it. We all have stories and some scars from our past experiences. These stories are our stories. We can see them as a negative experience or turn them into a positive learning opportunity. Use your past as a source of confidence, knowing you won't make the same mistake again; you won't let someone else define you; or, you'll adjust to new, different situations with grace, style, and confidence. Your past experiences hold potential to make you better within them. That is if you reframe them by shifting how you choose to reflect on them. Each experience is different and unique. Use your experience to motivate you to be a person who's grown from their past and is better for it.

Step Three: Surround Yourself with Positive People

When you surround yourself with positive people, you're more likely to adopt empowering beliefs. Create an inner circle of friends, co-workers, and relationships where you lift each other up, share knowledge, resources, and encouragement. Distance yourself from people who bring you down, are critical in a negative way, and have toxic attitudes. Surround yourself with motivated people who are ambitious. Seek out people willing to stretch themselves and open up to different perspectives and world views. The more positive you are the more likely you'll attract other positive people, and you'll be attracted to other positive people. This concept is often referred to as the *law of attraction.*

No one technique works all the time for everyone. As I've said throughout these pages, you're unique, and one size doesn't fit all. Your head voice can be a powerful tool to master motivation. It can boost confidence so you can perform at your absolute best. It's a superpower!

ACTIVITY #9

STOP LIVING IN THE SUFFOCATING SPACE OF SELF-THREAT AND EMERGE INTO THE SPACE OF SELF-MOTIVATION

As I noted earlier, researchers estimate we think about 50,000 to 70,000 thoughts a day and up to 80 percent of those thoughts are negative ones. Managing your head voice can lead you out of the suffocating space of self-threat so you can emerge into a space of self-motivation and achieve the success you deserve.

Apply steps one through three to build awareness, employ proactive techniques to manage your head voice, and surround yourself with positive people.

1. Catch your monkey when it jumps out of its basket. Acknowledge its effort to protect you and say thank you for sharing and caring. Now get back in your basket. Recognize focusing on negative, self-deprecating thoughts are self-destructive and lead to decreased motivation and feelings of loss and defeat.
2. When you have negative thoughts that create emotional states of fear, anger, anxiety, and shame, use at least one technique from this chapter or your own to shift your thinking from negative to positive. In the moment, recall what you're grateful for, and what you appreciate about your current situation. Take control of your thoughts.
3. Distance yourself as best you can from toxic people and spend more time with those who are uplifting, encouraging, and motivated. Be that uplifting, encouraging, and motivated person for others as well.

KEY CONCEPTS

- ✓ Your thoughts greatly influence how you feel and behave.
- ✓ Telling yourself you're not good enough over and over will eventually manifest into your truth. Your feelings of low self-worth will get in the way of achieving your goals.
- ✓ Negative self-talk links back to when we feared disapproval and rejection from caregivers, siblings, teachers, or other influential people in our lives.
- ✓ Negative self-talk stifles creativity, performance, and motivation.
- ✓ Scientists have discovered changing how you talk to yourself can free you from the space of suffocating in self-threat and emerge in a space of self-motivation.
- ✓ When your head voice is your *believer* and advocates for you, you feel as if you can achieve anything.
- ✓ Your head voice can be a powerful tool to master motivation. It can boost confidence that frees your mind so you can perform at your absolute best. It's a superpower!

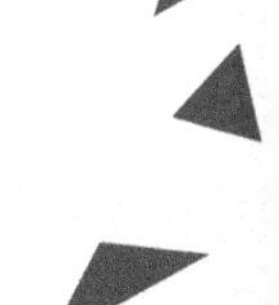

YOUR NOTES:

SHE BELIEVED SHE COULD, SO SHE DID

CHAPTER 10

Mastering Self-Motivation Breakthrough: Empowerment

Mandi's Journey to Discovering Her Superpower: Empowerment!

SEPTEMBER 15TH

Ring! Ring!

Mandi: "Hi Ann, this is Mandi."

Ann: "Hi Mandi. How are you today?"

Mandi: "Doing great. I couldn't be more excited about today's coaching call."

Ann: "That's wonderful! I can hear it in your voice. Tell me why? What are you excited about?"

Mandi: "Well, thanks to what I've learned in our coaching sessions, I've discovered how to master my own self-motivation. I've had a personal motivational breakthrough!! I've discovered my superpowers – I'm empowered!"

Ann: "Fantastic, Mandi. Tell me more."

Mandi: Well, I kept a journal of my experiences to discover my superpowers and mastered my self-motivation along the way. If it's okay with you, I'd like to share my story as it's evolved through our coaching sessions over the last few months."

Ann: "That sound perfect – do tell!"

Mandi's Journal

March 15th

After another holiday season full of celebrations came and went. Another year of fattening foods and high-calorie drinks under my belt, once again, I declared a New Year's resolution to lose weight and get in shape. My doc gave me the green light. I set a goal to lose two pounds a week. I recruited Marcy as my walking buddy. I hung my yellow silk dress with the tags still attached on the door for inspiration. What could go wrong? I got this! Right?

Sadly, my focus and enthusiasm waned. Marcy hurt her foot, so she can't be my conscious to keep me on track walking every day. Going back to work after the holidays didn't help either. I'm tempted by all the office goodies I shouldn't eat. Why are there donuts and pizza at work? Don't they understand how hard it is to resist?

I feel disengaged at work. I'm scrolling my social media to avoid getting work done. I need help. If I don't do something, I'll blow my diet, and I'll probably gain more weight. I'm bored. My interest and enthusiasm about my job is in the toilet. And if I don't get out of this rut and find some motivation, my job performance will suffer. I have a choice: quit and find a new job, stay in a rut, and maybe get fired, or get help.

I asked Marcy for advice. She said, "You're unmotivated. I know the perfect person to help you. Her name is Ann Holland. She's a motivation coach. Here's her number. Call her!" So, I did.

Today I called Ann. She seems nice enough. After telling her my story, she said she would help me if I was committed to helping myself. Okay fine, I'm committed! We set a coaching schedule. I'll call her every other week. We'll discuss what's going on. She'll share insights into how my brain works and how I can shift my thinking. That will shift how I behave and approach my job, relationships, and life.

She's going to give me assignments to help me find what works for me, since everyone's a little different. Ann suggested keeping a journal to capture my thoughts and to complete the activities or assignments. I've never kept a journal before, so this is a new experience. Ann will help me discover what she calls my superpowers to master my self-motivation. I'm open and ready to learn. I'm ready to power up my motivation!

Coaching Session 1: Power Up My Motivation

Ann asked me to consider what I want to get out of our sessions. She also asked me to start thinking about my life as an autobiographical documentary. She asked me to mull over what I'd entitle my documentary. I want to put serious thought into the idea. I want to dive into these questions in our next session. She suggested I start thinking about it now. Good questions. Questions I haven't spent much time thinking about.

After spending quiet time contemplating what I want from my career and my life, I've decided, I want purpose. I want to rise every day and feel good about my life and myself. I want pep in my step as I head out the door and meet the day. I want to:

- Contribute to the world in a positive way.
- Be a better person tomorrow than I am today.
- Progress in my career.
- Live a healthier lifestyle.
- Deepen my spiritual walk with God.
- Have a healthy relationship with my husband and family.

So, in our sessions I want help setting my

path and staying on course. More than anything, I need to discover how to tap into my gifts, talents, and purpose. I also want to find an inner source of inspiration and motivation to drive and sustain me. I want to figure out how to pull my motivation from within, so I don't have to rely on others to inspire or motivate me to achieve my goals. I want to know how to overcome barriers and stifle my incessant inner chatter. It only brings me down and gets in the way of what I truly want.

I'm on board and ready to get started!

Activity #1: Self Awareness

What motivates me? My top three motivational factors are:

1. Purpose: (score = 10). Purpose is having internal meaning to what I do. It can include leaving a legacy, altruism-helping others, having a positive impact or driving change, being relevant, self-actualization, or finding enlightenment.

2. Personal success: (score = 8). Personal success is about fulfilling desires related to my lifestyle, values, and belief systems. It can include balance, family time, having a sense of security and stability, being my personal best,

independence, or simply experiencing peace and happiness.

3. Relatedness: (score =7). Relatedness is connection to others in a positive way. It's social connectivity, feeling of acceptance, a sense of belonging, and attachment to others, teams, projects, or movements.

How do I get in my way? The top three areas where I get stuck include:

1. Distractors. I scroll my social media, news feeds, or let other distractors get in the way of completing work.
2. Lack of goals. Maybe with goals and an intentional plan for strategic growth, I'd stay on course better.
3. Lack of confidence. I let my inner critic dominate my thoughts when I consider trying new things.

This was a helpful activity. I never gave much thought to what motivates me or how I get in my way. After identifying my top three motivations and barriers, I can be more mindful and focused as I develop my skills and achieve my goals. I look forward to the next step.

Coaching Session 2: What is Motivation Anyway?

Finding my personal source of inspiration and motivation.

1. Where do I find my energy?

I love the energy I feel around animals. Their unconditional love lights a flame in my heart and brings me joy. I could spend every day working with animals.

2. What excites me?

When I notice how excited my dog, Lady, is to see me when I get home from work. As much as I hate admitting it, she's equally as excited to see my husband, Don, when he comes home from work. Honestly, Lady wags her tail and rolls-over exposing her underside for a belly rub whenever she comes across a person she senses appreciates and cares for her or animals in general. It makes my day, when I see the joy she brings others as well as the joy she feels. I have the same experience when I visit mom. Her cats, Sparky, Shorty, and Max, run to see me for a quick hello, a few kisses, and strokes to the tail.

3. What's my purpose?

This is the million-dollar question. As I think about it, I believe my skills, talents, gifts, and passion pull me toward helping animals and people, specifically elderly people. Until Don started working in a long-term care and rehabilitation facility, and I started caring for my elderly parents, I never knew or appreciated how lonely life can be for an elderly person who's not surrounded by family or friends. Many days go by when they don't talk to anyone; or, it may just be a brief encounter with a volunteer delivering Meals on Wheels; or, in the nursing home, the overworked, stressed-out nurse who drops off their meds and barely spends enough time to ensure they swallow their pills. I feel passionate about animals and elderly people. Somewhere therein lies my purpose. I haven't taken time or put energy into figuring it out.

4. If I had no obstacles in my way, what would I do?

- If I had no worries about resources, I'd come up with a program which allows animals to visit elderly people in nursing homes or private homes. The connection between elderly people and animals is undeniable, however, many seniors may not feel they can safely care for an animal. Many seniors are afraid to adopt a dog or cat because they can't physically tend to them or afford their care. Some avoid adopting an animal because they fear their life could end before their pet's life, and they don't want to leave a beloved pet to an uncertain future. That would break their heart.
- I just had an epiphany! Inspiration! I never

thought it through before. I want to create a non-profit that brings dogs and cats to visit homebound elderly people as well as those in nursing homes. I'm excited about this idea. Now I just need to figure out how to do it!

5. What do I value most in my career or life?

Suddenly, this question is easy. I value helping others thrive.

Activity #2: Self-Awareness:

Imagine you're living your best career/life!

What is my vision for my career or life? Describe in detail what it looks like:

I'm the founder and CEO of the non-profit organization: Pets with Purpose. I have a staff of trained volunteers who visit nursing homes, assisted living centers, private homes, and other facilities providing pet love and therapy. My pet companionship program provides pet-friendly visits bringing dogs, cats, rabbits, and other suitable pets to seniors who enjoy interacting with animals.

Describe how I feel:

Anyone who sees the wag of a happy dog's tail, strokes the soft fur of a rabbit, or hears and feels the gentle rumble of a cat's purr knows the calming feelings an animal offers. Knowing I'm enhancing the life of an ailing, lonely, or depressed senior by providing a positive mental, emotional, and often physical benefit will be so fulfilling, it's indescribable. I'll feel I have purpose. It will give me:

- A reason to get up every day and feel good about my life and myself.
- That pep in my step as I go out and meet each day.
- A feeling I'm contributing to the world in a positive way.
- An opportunity to be a better person tomorrow than I am today.
- A career, a life, and a way to feed my passion.
- A deeper spiritual walk with God because I'm doing God's work.
- An opportunity to use the talents and gifts that God blessed me with.
- The inspiration and motivation to move forward, pursuing my dream.

In my best career/life as I've described it, what do I value most?

- I value people. I'll lead my paid staff and volunteers with care, respect, and direction so they feel excited and energized to bring animals and people together safely and enthusiastically.

- I value the elderly. I've observed many elderly people who feel lonely, depressed, and suffer ailments that might improve if their mental, emotional, and physical state was better. Love and especially the unconditional love of an animal will provide feelings of belonging and being cared for, which is often missing in their lives.
- I value my husband and family. I will be a happier, better person when I'm doing what I was put here to do and follow my dreams.
- I value my health. I'm more motivated to get in better shape and live a healthier life. Suddenly, avoiding donuts and pizza to wear that yellow dress doesn't drive me. Now, it's about being in great shape to live my best life. I want the physical, mental, and emotional energy to get up every day and work on planning and preparing for and ultimately living my best career and life.

In my best career/life, what drivers, needs, or desires are satisfied?

Realizing my dream career, my need to belong, and have purpose and a sense of internal meaning will be satisfied. My desire to help others, make a positive impact, and drive change as well as be relevant and experience self-actualization will be met.

When I act on what drives me, I'll experience career success. My personal success will be a result of fulfilling my desires, living according to my values and beliefs. I'm driven by a need to belong to a team or movement. Pursuing my dream career will take me to a place where I feel connected and productive. I'll move the personal world of those in need to a better place. That's a movement!

Write the title to my autobiography:

"Mandi Rescues People and Pets!"

This activity helped me discover my passion from a deeper place. It triggered my inspiration and motivation, energizing me to move forward with purpose bringing meaning to my career and life.

Coaching Session 3: How Motivation Works.

I now have a better understanding of how motivation works using both my brain and my mind. I feel empowered to change my behavior and develop new habits. Looking forward to trying it out.

Activity #3: Steps to Creating a New Neuropathway

Using the SMART Goal-setting Guide: Specific, Measurable, Attainable, Relevant, Timebound— set long-term, mid-term, and short-term goals.

- **Long-term goal:** Establish a non-profit "Pets with Purpose" companion program, bringing suitable animals to visit seniors in my community in the next five years.
- **Mid-term goal:** Develop skills in leadership, project management, and business through training and experience with my current employer as well as enrolling in external programs.
- **Short-term goals:** Read at least two articles or one book per month and participate in one virtual training or work-related training focused on leadership development, team building, project management, or business acumen in the non-profit space per quarter.

The three behaviors I'll work on: what I'll stop doing, start doing, and continue doing. How will I feel? What value do I assign to the behavior? What trigger will I use? How will this satisfy my desires and needs?

Behavior	How will I feel?	What value do I put on this behavior (1-10)
Stop: Scrolling social media.	More productive and focused on my work and long-term goals.	10
Start: Seeking opportunity to mentor or be mentored.	I'll be spending time working on building my skills. A good feeling. Progress!	10
Continue: Do my current job with the intention of learning and growing as opportunity allows.	I like my job and those with whom I work. I'll enjoy my team and the job I do.	10

I'll begin working on these three behaviors this week. To reinforce my behavior, I'll check in with myself weekly and reflect on my progress. If I have more thumbs up than thumbs down on my self-assessment, I'll feel good about my success and reward myself with a pampering moment. Maybe I'll take a bubble bath, do my nails, or take a long meditative nature walk. I'm committed to acknowledging my progress

What trigger will I use?	How will this satisfy my needs/desires
Turn off my phone when it is time to focus on work. Have specific time to catch up with texts and phone calls.	I won't be wasting time. I'll be working toward my goals.
Review the skills I'd like to develop quarterly. Decide which skills to focus on.	I'll develop new skills and fine-tune skills to prepare me for my long-term goals.
Pause when I feel stressed or anxious. Be present. Listen and learn with intention, knowing this is an opportunity to learn and grow my skills.	Practice pausing, listening, and learning will prepare me as a leader and non-profit owner.

with a reward that feels good. If I have more thumbs down than thumbs up, I'll reflect on what got in my way and see what I can adjust to improve my progress.

I look forward to my next coaching call. I'm excited about my plan to work toward achieving my goals by retraining my brain and working on the behaviors that matter most. I'm excited to share my thoughts with Ann.

Coaching Session 4: Mastering Your Mindset

Wow! What an insightful discussion with Ann on mastering my mindset. Where do I begin? A lot to unpack from today's session. I think I'll extract some nuggets that resonate with me most and where I'm at in my head now.

I think I'm a positive person. I can't wait to learn and try new things. I especially like the notion my mindset and inner chatter can limit or liberate me. I feel empowered to be who I want to be. I'm sticking with my mantra, "I want to be a better person tomorrow than I am today." I can do it if I pay attention to my mindset. I feel I can do anything I set my mind to accomplish.

I smile at the idea of being an observer of my beliefs, assumptions, and thoughts. I'll take the next two weeks to observe my mindset. I'm going to take note of when I'm thinking positively and how I feel in those moments, and when I fall into the trap of negative or victim mindset and how I feel in those moments. I'll pause and reflect when I make assumptions about situations, people, and myself. I'll observe my language, noting if it's positive or negative; especially, when I hear my self-talk wreaking havoc. It's my mind and my choice what I believe, how I see the world, and how I see myself.

I like the affirmation, "I'm showing up as my best self today!" I'll write it on a post-it-note and stick it on my bathroom mirror to create a mindset trigger. Then I'll write a reminder to be my own coach: I'll observe, pause, reflect, and act to be my best self.

Coaching Session 5 and 6: The Emotional Brain & Growing Your Emotional Intelligence

Today was my first opportunity to mentor a colleague. It was awesome sharing what I discovered about how to use my brain's capacity to manage my emotions. It's only been three weeks since attending Ann's workshop on The Emotional Brain, when my colleague, Sam, needed help. He had a meltdown, or what Ann refers to as an "emotional hijacking," after his boss said the company was going in a different direction, and the project he and his team worked on had to be sidelined. I mentored Sam back to a bit more emotional stability.

I explained we're emotional creatures. It's understandable he'd react spontaneously when his limbic system was triggered by a situation he perceived as threatening, causing a fight, flight, or freeze response. The adrenaline shoots through the body like pent up lava spewing from a volcano that's laid dormant too long. It feels like you have no control, but it's awesome knowing you do have control over your response to emotional triggers. I explained Sam's emotional triggers are embedded in his memory due to past experiences. The good news is if he can resist a knee-jerk reaction, pause, observe, think, shift his mindset with intention, and respond in a way that puts him in a growth mindset, he'll tap into his superpowers.

Learning to shift my mindset and manage my emotions has been a game changer. Once I explained to Sam how emotional intelligence works and how he can learn to manage his emotions, he was able to see the event as an opportunity to show his leadership skills. He was able to use emotional intelligence to develop his self-motivation and move forward.

I really got Sam's attention when I told him, EI is an essential competency in leadership roles. The value and benefits of emotional intelligence is in forming and developing meaningful relationships as well as managing your psychological health. I shared with Sam information that I came across that was put out by The Center for Creative Leadership about how careers are derailed for reasons related to emotional competencies, including inability to handle interpersonal problems; unsatisfactory team leadership during times of difficulty or conflict; or inability to adapt to change or elicit trust. Organizations are recognizing the value of employees who exhibit the skills essential to adapt to change, accept constructive feedback with a growth mindset, and work effectively with a team. Sam was really on board when I told him 90 percent of high performers are also high in EQ and almost always make more money.

The bottom line is EI is an important factor in job performance on an individual level as well as with your team. This was an important lesson for Sam and me. As I grow into leadership roles, leading a team in my current job as well as my future leading my non-profit, growing my emotional quotient will be critical to success.

Coaching Session 7: Well-Being Effects on Motivation

I'm so glad we're discussing health and fitness. After all, this is how everything got started. I felt sluggish, struggling with brain fog, lacking motivation, and wanted to lose a few pounds. Drinking gallons of coffee and scrolling social media to avoid work wasn't getting me anywhere. If my brain's out of whack, my body will be out of whack. If my body is out of whack, my brain will be out of whack. It's the "chicken or the egg" conundrum.

Now that I know how my brain works, I can retrain it to think differently. I can change old ways of thinking and break bad habits by switching off old neuropathways which don't serve me. I'll switch on new neuropathways by making better choices. Having a healthy mind, body, and spirit is important to mastering my motivation.

Activity #7 Establishing Healthy Habits

First: Prioritize the most important changes you want or need to make. You don't have to do them all at once. Start with one change at a time if you prefer. I want:

- More energy, eliminating the brain fog that clouds my focus.
- To get toned and closer to a healthier BMI, losing five to ten pounds.
- Sustain my motivation to work toward my long-term goal of establishing my "Pets with Purpose" non-profit.

Second: Establish the habit. What will you do differently to make change? How will it benefit you? What process can you put in place to implement change?

Third: Getting Support. Who can you enlist? What system can you put in place to support you in making a change?

Getting Healthy

BRAIN, BODY, AND SPIRIT

Habit	Cues	Support System
	First Habit	
Turn off electronic devices 30 minutes before going to bed, journal the three things I'm grateful for instead of watching TV or scrolling on my phone. Using a daily devotional will also help me keep my spiritual devotion on my mind and in my heart as I start and end my day.	Lay my daily devotional journal on my pillow after I make the bed in the morning, so I pick it up when I get in bed at night. Put my phone in the top drawer of my nightstand so I don't see it light up.	Inform my family and friends I won't take calls (unless it's a real emergency) or respond to emails, texts, or other communications after 9:00 pm. This will give me quiet time to clear my mind and sleep better.
	Second Habit	
Each morning I get out of bed and stretch with a 30 minute yoga flow practice with music. This is good for mind, body, and spirit. It'll help me reduce brain fog and get ready for the day.	Mount a yoga flow poster on the wall where I do my practice, so I see it every morning staring back at me.	Re-engage with my yoga coach. Meet once every two weeks as a check-in and to brush up on my practice.

	Third Habit	
Take Lady for a 30-minute jog/ walk after work to decompress from the hustle and bustle of the day. This provides aerobic activity as well.	Lady's my cue. She needs no help learning a new habit, especially if she gets a walk.	Lady is my support system for this activity. She loves me unconditionally, but she loves me more when we go walking!
	Fourth Habit	
Plan meals. I make a weekly list for the grocery store already. No reason I can't do a better job planning our meals.	Keep shopping list on kitchen counter to jot down items. Keep a healthy cookbook nearby to quickly look up recipes and stay on track.	Share healthy recipes with family and friends. Who knows, I may start a movement with family and friends to eat healthier.

Fourth: Acknowledge your progress. Reflect on your progress, celebrate your accomplishments, or adjust behaviors, as necessary.

As part of journaling, I'll reflect on my progress, acknowledge my success, and adjust my behaviors. At least once a month, I'll volunteer at the animal shelter or an elderly care facility to keep my enthusiasm and motivation up. This celebration makes me feel good and keeps me on track with my purpose!

Coaching Session 8: Mental Performance

Activity #8 Breaking the Boredom Barrier

Once again, Ann has given me plenty to think about and digest. Sometimes I feel bored at work. I'm sure that is why I'm so easily distracted and have a hard time staying on task. After reflecting on why I feel bored, I realize one of the biggest issues is I'm not working toward a goal that I feel passionate about. I like my job just fine. However, I am not passionate about it. Now that I'm inspired about what I want to do with my life long-term, I can create a plan to develop the skills I need to build my own business.

Setting small goals will help me feel challenged, learn, and stretch my comfort zone. It will give me the opportunity to practice a positive growth mindset. Establishing achievable milestones will also help me cultivate the discipline to concentrate on the daily tasks knowing that I'm building a set of skills that will help me in my current job and prepare me for the future. Ann suggested, when my mind begins to wander, train my brain to focus on the task in front of me, while I visualize my longer-term purpose. She calls it, having bifocal vision. It's important to remind myself that today's experience is paving the way to realizing tomorrow's dream.

To help me stay energized about my goals, I

am going to volunteer to visit the homebound members of my church on the weekends. This will feed my purpose. It will also give meaning to what I am doing at work to develop my skills. As Ann says, "Keep your eye on the prize!"

Coaching Session 9: Your Head Voice

Am I getting in my own way? My monkey mind went ape when I asked myself this question. I never realized how hard I've been on myself over the years. I can be and have been both my worst enemy and my best friend.

I guess I've always known I talk to myself but never realized the power of self-talk. The negative thoughts in my head aren't facts, they're just thoughts. Allowing myself to hear the monkey mind chatter in the moment is okay, but then, it's up to me and only me to send the monkey back to her basket and replace the negative chatter with thoughts that are more like the things I'd say to encourage and support my best friend.

As I practice catching those negative thoughts, shifting my thought patterns by reframing the situation as a positive experience, I've found I'm a happier person, more pleasant to be around, and definitely more motivated. I think about chasing lightening bugs as a kid. You see it, you capture it in a jar, notice it for its purpose (in this case my monkey mind is just trying to protect me), and then, let it go! I'm pretty sure out of all the lessons I've learned in this journey of finding my superpowers to becoming self-motivated, this is the most powerful! Let's face it, negative self-talk won't get me where I want to be. Having a growth mindset and a positive best friend as my head voice will help me realize my dream of having my own business, "Pets with Purpose!"

I've learned a lot from this journey and my coaching sessions with Ann. Most importantly, I realize I have superpowers that come from within. I don't have to rely on anyone else to inspire me or motivate me. I can do this!

And, you can do this too!

CONCLUSION

The Turning Point

It's May 1st, I open my eyes, squint, blink a few times to bring the digital numbers on the cable box across the room that serves as a platform for our TV into focus. It says 5:03 AM or is it 5:08 AM. I'm not sure yet, because my eyes are still blurry, and the room is dark. The air in the room is cool, fresh, and carries the aroma of recently cut grass as it wafts in from the open windows. It is a welcome spring morning, after a never-ending overcast, bone-chilling winter. The flutelike songs of robins, sparrows, and finches serve as a natural alarm clock whose purpose is to greet the new day. It takes great energy to sing so loudly and with such power. The aviary dawn chorus is a phenomenon, which starts as early as four in the morning at my house and lasts for hours. Listening to their songs always lifts my spirit.

I think about what possibly motivates birds to sing every morning without fail with such passion and desire. The birds tucked in the trees nearby are driven by an intrinsic push to show off their vocal prowess each morning demonstrating the singer is both strong and healthy. Their refrain is an appeal compelled by a need to find a new mate or renew a bond with an existing one. The birds use their natural abilities to send a message to a pool of potential mates, letting them clearly know they're fit enough to survive a night of dipping temperatures and active predators. For birds, their motivation and ritual are driven by a need to mate and an effort to claim their territory.

My motivation this day is to bring a message to an audience that could change their lives. I'm facilitating my first seminar on Self-Motivation Mastery. The realization that I've finished my book and am ready to present my first seminar on the topic shoots adrenaline through my body and awakens the butterflies in my stomach. I can almost feel them stretch their wings, yawn, and rub the winkies from their little eyes. Yes, butterflies have two eyes just as we do. They have compound eyes because they have many lenses. That means butterflies can see many different things in many directions all at the same time. No doubt, butterflies can teach us a few lessons.

I spring from bed and head to the kitchen with my dog following on my heels. As soon as the butterflies settle down, I make a hearty breakfast because I know I'll need the fuel a nutritious breakfast provides for my big day.

As I sit on my porch sipping my morning coffee, I can hear the groan of my monkey mind begin to churn as it wakes up as well. It doesn't take long before the chatter begins. "Here we go, this is your big day. How will it go? Will people show up? Will they like the seminar? Will they think they wasted their money? Will they like me? What should I wear? What if there's an accident on the freeway, and I'm late? Maybe I should leave earlier?"

Stop! Pause! "Thank you for sharing, I know you're only trying to protect me, but I got this!" I fire back. I take control of my thoughts and reframe my perspective. "I've been preparing for this moment for a long time. I've done the research. I'm qualified, experienced, and passionate about the message I bring. This is who I am. This is my purpose. Those who signed up are there for a reason."

The stage is set, the room is full, and the audience settles into their seats. I had the opportunity to meet a few participants at the breakfast bar, while they were grabbing a few snacks to keep their growling stomachs from drawing attention to them while I'm speaking. I met two young women who recently graduated from law school and are hoping to open a family law practice. I also met several business leaders, entrepreneurs, students, and a few coaches who signed up hoping to discover a few new tools they can use to help their clients master their self-motivation. There were people from various professions, representing a spectrum of generations, and in different phases of their life's journey. Each person has their own story and purpose for attending. Each person is completely unique, like you, so finding and mastering their motivation is a personal path of self-discovery.

SELF-MOTIVATION IS NOT COOKIE-CUTTER

Self-motivation is not cookie-cutter. Find what works for you. However, what we know as a commonality among all of us is the entire process starts in the brain. Your brain has specific switches that trigger certain thoughts and actions. Now that you're beginning to understand:

- how your brain works
- how your mind works, and,
- most importantly, how they work together,

you can now make a more conscious effort to gain control of your thoughts and feelings. You're empowered with the knowledge you can literally change the programming and chemistry in your brain. So, you have the tools and the power within your brain to become self-motivated.

Professional success begins with personal growth, rooted in self-discovery, changing your thoughts, behaviors, and establishing new habits. As you practice the activities outlined in this book that resonate with you, the more you'll successfully shift so you control your thoughts and behaviors. As you do, you strengthen new neuropathways, cementing new habits into your conscious and subconscious mind. The person who has the greatest power to change you is you.

The concepts in this book don't work in isolation. They're inextricably linked and using them in concert is another superpower. The benefits of discovering your superpowers don't end with motivation. As you develop your superpowers, you'll attract people with like mindsets to your inner circle, perpetuating motivation and positivity. Motivation is contagious. Your positive mindset and behavior will have a ripple effect on friends, colleagues, and your circle of influence. By changing how you think and behave you can change the world, at least your part of the world.

Our emotions are enormously contagious as well. Using the concepts of emotional intelligence, you now know you possess the ability to manage your emotions and influence others by how you handle situations. Daniel Goleman said, "Like secondhand smoke, the leakage of emotions can make a bystander an innocent casualty of someone else's toxic state." When you feel anxious or are in a negative mindset, these emotions can seep into every interaction at work or in your personal life, whether you intend it or not. Everyone's had the experience of walking into a meeting when the tension is thick, and the mood is like a heavy wet blanket. Fortunately, positive emotions work the same way, which make them a superpower in creating a positive high performance work team or work environment.

I've shared examples of people who discovered and applied their personal superpowers. Whether it's Tiger Woods who set his intention to be the world's best golfer, or Oprah Winfrey's commitment to live life through the lens of a positive mindset, each story is unique to their circumstances, just as your story, needs, and desires are unique to you. The common thread in each story is their personal pledge to be a better person tomorrow than they are today. Successful people find and sustain success as a result of a lifelong journey of self-discovery. The process is continuous. My hope is what you've discovered in this book about yourself and your superpowers has provided you with the tools and confidence to feel equipped and empowered to become your best self and accomplish what you've always dreamed of accomplishing.

YOU GOT THIS!

RESOURCES

Books

Arden, J. B. (2010). *Rewire Your Brain: Think Your Way to a Better Life.* Hoboken, NJ, John Wiley & Sons.

Carmona, R. (2014). *30 Days to a Better Brain.* New York, NY, Atria Books.

Compton, W. C., & Hoffman, E. (2013). *Positive Psychology: The Science of Happiness and Flourishing.* Belmont, CA. Wadsworth Cengage Learning.

Davidson, R., & Begley, S. (2012). *The Emotional Life of Your Brain.* Hudson Street Press.

Deckers, L. (2018). *Motivation: Biological, Psychological, and Environmental, 5th Edition.* New York, NY. Routledge.

Doidge, N. (2007). *The Brain that Changes Itself: Stories of Personal Triumph from the Frontiers of Brain Science.* New York, NY, Penguin Books.

Dweck, C. S. (2006). *Mindset.* New York, NY, Random House Publishing Group.

Fredrickson, B. L. (2009). *Positivity.* New York, NY, MJF Books.

Goleman, D. (1994). *Emotional Intelligence.* New York, NY, Bantam Dell.

Gottfredson, R. (2020). *Successful Mindsets: Your Keys to Unlocking Greater Success in Your Life, Work, & Leadership.* New York, NY, Morgan James Publishing.

Gottfried, S. (2019). *Brain Body Diet: 40 days to a Lean, Calm, Energized, and Happy Self.* New York, NY, HarperCollins Publishing.

Jacobs, D. (2017). *Banish Your Inner Critic: Silence the Voice of Self-Doubt to Unleash Your Creativity and Do Your Best Work.* Mango Publishing.

Neff, K., & Germer, C. (2018). *The Mindful Self-Compassion Workbook.* New York, NY, Guildford Press.

Piaget, J. (1950). *Piaget: The Psychology of Intelligence.* New York, NY, Routledge.

Seth, A. (2012). *30-Second Brain: The 50 Most Mind-Blowing Ideas in Neuroscience, Each Explained in Half a Minute.* New York, NY, Ivy Press

Limited.

Walton, D. (2012). *Emotional Intelligence: A Practical Guide.* New York, NY, MJF Books.

Magazines

Hayes, S. "Why You Focus on The Wrong Things." *Psychology Today.* August 2019. pp. 38-40.

Pincott, J. "Silence Your Inner Critic." *Psychology Today*. April 2019. pp. 50-57.

Weintraub, P. "The Voice of Reason." *Psychology Today*. June 2015. pp. 53-59.

ACKNOWLEDGEMENTS

I have yearned to write a book for a very long time. I have had a million ideas, lists of titles, and a few outlines for chapter headings. However, I have never been able to get out of the gate and actually start writing. I always put my dream of writing a book on the back burner.

In 2020, I hired a coach to help me launch a podcast. I thought this would be a wise way to get my message out to the world. Well, it turns out, after brilliant coaching, we got to the core of what I really wanted to do and that was write a book. Thank you Wendy Green for your incredible coaching and giving me the confidence to get out of the gate.

Being a coach myself, I know how valuable coaches are. Since this was my first book, I knew I would need a book coach to guide me through the process. Wendy referred me to Denise Michaels. I interviewed Denise. I knew from her previous experience and the way we interacted she was the right coach for me. She held my feet to the fire, she pushed and pulled me in different directions, and we got there.

Over the years, I have had a few mentors who helped stretch me and allowed me the space to reach my potential. Like good coaches, good mentors are important. They not only support and encourage you, but they also push and pull you to move out of your comfort zone, expanding your abilities and confidence. I would like to take this opportunity to thank a few of the mentors who helped me throughout my career and educational journey: Richard Schuetz (CEO, Schuetz, LLC), Dr. Barbara Mink (Dean, School of Leadership Studies, Fielding Graduate University), Tom Lippie (retired, formerly President, Client First Associates), and Liz Parker (Owner, LT Consultants).

Parents are an interesting dynamic in your life. They love you and raise you the best they know. As my mom always says, "God did not give me a manual when he blessed me with my five children. I did the best I could with what I had and what I knew." My mom, Beatrice Florence Geer, is my parent, mentor, coach, prayer warrior, biggest challenge at times, and best friend. I miss my dad, John Rook, very much. However, I know he is looking down from heaven and is very proud, as he was always proud of me and told me so many times throughout my life.

My heavenly father walks with me through the thick and thin of life here on earth. He allows me to fail and succeed; struggle and triumph; cry out in anguish and frustration; laugh with a joy-filled heart; and feel humbled and loved. He has sent his Son to pay the ultimate price, so I can live in His Kingdom, for that I am forever grateful.

The most important person in my life is my husband, Ron. We have been married more than twenty wonderful years. He has been the best thing that ever happened to me. He is steadfast, while I'm bouncing off the walls. He has been the calm that has gotten me through many storms in my life. I would not be doing the thing I love most and living the life I imagined if it were not for the love and support that I receive from Ron.

I would also like to acknowledge the researchers, scientists, scholars, and practitioners that continue to collect, analyze, synthesize, and publish information that help all of us be a better person tomorrow than we are today. All we have to do is find our inner motivation to take advantage of the information out there and apply it.

Finally, I would like to thank you, my readers. Thank you for taking a chance on an unknown author to take you on this journey of self-discovery to mastering your motivation. I wish you much success as you pursue and live the life you imagine.

ABOUT THE AUTHOR:

Ann Holland, PhD., born, Clara Ann Rook, in Philadelphia, Pennsylvania, grew up with four siblings and a German Shepard named Sarge. Ann (as she goes by her middle name) left the Philadelphia area at age twenty-five and never looked back. After moving across the country and living in eight different states, she is now settled in Greenville, South Carolina with her husband, Ron, and dog, Jena.

A seasoned professional with over 25 years of experience in leadership, organizational development, and learning and development, Ann holds a doctorate degree in Human Development; two master's degrees, one in Organizational Management, the other in Organizational Development; and a bachelor's degree in Business.

Holding many senior level leadership positions, Ann has experience in a variety of industries such as oil & gas, manufacturing, retail, entertainment, and hospitality. In addition, she teaches as an adjunct professor. She is an International Coaching Federation certified performance coach, an experience consultant, a member of the Forbes Coaches Council, and a regular contributor to Forbes.com.

Ann is the owner of Strive Performance Coaching and Consulting, working with organizations, teams, and individuals to reach performance objectives. Using the platform of Conscious Development, she created the STRIVE Performance Model. The STRIVE Performance model serves as a guide to develop emerging talent, building confidence and competence in key professional development areas. It is her passion and commitment to helping people with their personal and professional development that prompted Ann to write Self-Motivation Mastery.

To learn more about Strive Performance Coaching, or to order this book or related training material visit:

https://striveperformancecoaching.com/

Made in the USA
Coppell, TX
24 January 2022